CRIMINAL RESPONSIBILITY EVALUATIONS

A MANUAL FOR PRACTICE

David L. Shapiro, PhD

Professional Resource Press
Sarasota, Florida

Published by
Professional Resource Press
(An imprint of the Professional Resource Exchange, Inc.)
Post Office Box 15560
Sarasota, FL 34277-1560

Printed in the United States of America

The copy editor for this book was Judith Warinner, the managing editor was Debra Fink, the production coordinator was Laurie Girsch, the typesetter was Denise Franck, and the cover was created by Jami S. Stinnet.

Library of Congress Cataloging-in-Publication Data

Shapiro, David L., date.
    Criminal responsibility evaluations : a manual for practice / David L. Shapiro.
        p. cm.
    Includes bibliographical references and index.
    ISBN 1-56887-046-9 (alk. paper)
    1. Criminal liability--United States. 2. Insanity--Jurisprudence--United States. 3. Forensic psychiatry--United States. I. Title.
KF9235.S52 1999
345.73'04--dc21   98-54690
                                           CIP

ACKNOWLEDGMENTS

It is difficult to acknowledge all the people whose ideas have helped shape mine, and whose thought-provoking comments about various topics in forensic psychology have helped reshape mine. At the risk then of omitting certain key people, I will acknowledge my colleagues in forensic psychology, past, present and future.

<u>DEDICATION</u>

This book is dedicated in loving memory to my father, Frank Shapiro, and to his grandchildren, of whom he was so proud, Sara, Laura, Ann, and Jonathan.

PREFACE

Prior to the mid-1970s, psychologists (and, in fact, psychiatrists as well) who testified frequently in court were described as "hired guns" and in other terminology suggestive of the world's oldest profession. Over the course of the past 20 years, forensic psychology and psychiatry have become respected and distinct specialty areas. The quantity of research in the area has been phenomenal, as has the development of practice standards. Specific Codes of Ethics and Specialty Standards have been developed by both psychiatry and psychology[1, 2, 3] and rigorous Board certification examinations now exist in both disciplines. The most recent Code of Ethics of The American Psychological Association (1992) has a special section on forensic areas that did not exist previously. Writers who maintain that forensic experts have no data, no research and no standards of practice to back up their opinions in court are simply ignoring what has transpired in the past two decades.

Thomas Grisso wrote a manual dealing with issues of competency to stand trial and waivers of Miranda rights.[4] The current book is an attempt to provide a parallel practice manual for the area of criminal responsibility.

Criminal responsibility law, sometimes referred to as "M.S.O." (mental state at the time of the offense), is an area often misunder-

---

[1] American Psychological Association. (1992). Ethical Principles of Psychologists and Code of Conduct. *American Psychologist, 47*(12), 1597-1611.

[2] American Psychiatric Association. (1993). *The Principles of Medical Ethics With Annotations Especially Applicable to Psychiatry.* Washington, DC: Author.

[3] Specialty Guidelines for Forensic Psychologists. (1991). *Law and Human Behavior, 15*(6), 655-665.

[4] Grisso, T. (1988). *Competency to Stand Trial Evaluations: A Manual for Practice.* Sarasota, FL: Professional Resource Exchange.

stood by the public, misreported in the media and misquoted, sometimes even by attorneys and judges. This book will attempt to address and clarify some of these misunderstandings.

David L. Shapiro
Baltimore, Maryland
January, 1999

TABLE OF CONTENTS

CRIMINAL RESPONSIBILITY EVALUATIONS

A MANUAL FOR PRACTICE

Chapter 1

INTRODUCTION*

The question might arise, after many years of forensic clinicians doing criminal responsibility evaluations, is there a need for a practice manual. A variety of mental health clinicians, psychiatrists, psychologists and social workers, have been rendering opinions regarding a person's mental state at the time of an offense. Over the years, as the area of forensic mental health assessment has become more well-defined, some consensus has arisen regarding the manner in which these evaluations are performed. That is, the initial impression of the psychiatrist, psychologist or social worker who sits down, interviews a patient and, without any further input, renders an opinion regarding mental state at the time of the offense, has given way to a far more sophisticated approach in which the clinician realizes that the clinical examination is only one piece of a much larger puzzle. It has now been recognized in virtually all writings and all textbooks on the subject that criminal responsibility evaluations must represent an integration of multiple data sources looking at the consistencies across those data sources. In other words, beginning with a clinical interview, the forensic clinician will generate certain hypotheses which will be refined and, in some instances, discarded, as the evaluation proceeds. Each hypothesis will, in essence, be tested out against other sources of data such as the psychological testing, the police reports, the witness' statements, the hospital records, the employment records and so on. What emerges as the final product will be that which is consistent across a variety

---

* Appendix F (pp. 157-160) lists publishers and distributors of some of the psychological instruments and other materials discussed in this book. Appendix G (pp. 161-167) contains a glossary of many of the terms used in this book that may be unfamiliar to some readers.

1

of data sources. There have been, in fact, several cases recently in which testimony has not been admitted because the clinician failed to investigate these secondary sources of data.[1, 2]

What has developed over the course of many years is a generally accepted standard regarding how criminal forensic assessments are to be done. What is in the process of being solidified, in other words, is a "standard of care" for performing such assessments. Standard of care is most often defined as the level of practice exercised by the average or relatively prudent professional. The concept is most often applicable in the context of malpractice litigation, that is, did the provider or practitioner in some way deviate from an accepted standard of care, and did a harm or injury result directly from that deviation from the standard of care (the concept of proximate cause). Although it is unlikely that someone performing a criminal responsibility evaluation would become the defendant in a malpractice action regarding her or his conduct of the assessment, the concept of a standard of care in performing such evaluations is an important one to be kept in mind.

FRYE VS. UNITED STATES*

In a landmark case more than 70 years ago,[3] the Court of Appeals of the District of Columbia decided on December 3, 1923 what the criteria for the admissibility of expert testimony needed to

---

* **Note regarding legal citations.** Throughout this book, the reader will encounter references to legal cases. For those unfamiliar with legal citations, the following brief comments may help to clarify the references. Most states and federal jurisdictions have what are called Law Reporters, books in which appellate decisions are reprinted. The Supreme Court of the United States also has its own series of reports. The Law Reporters may be N.E. (Northeast), S.E. (Southeast) or a variety of other areas or states (e.g., CAL RPTR would be the Law Reporter for the State of California).

The name of the case will appear first, followed by the volume number, the name of the Reporter, the page number where the decision begins, and the Court from which it originated. For instance, someone interested in looking up *Strozier vs. Georgia*, 334 S.E. 2d 181 (Ga. S.Ct. 1985) would look for Volume 334 of the Second Edition of the Southeast Reporter, text beginning on Page 181. The case was one handed down by the Supreme Court of the State of Georgia.

Someone interested in looking up *Illinois vs. Smith*, 464 N.E. 2d 685 (Ill. Ct. App. 1984) would look for Volume 464 of the Second Edition of the Northeast Reporter, text beginning on Page 685. The case was handed down by the Illinois Court of Appeals in 1984.

---

[1] *Strozier vs. Georgia*, 334 S.E. 2d 181 (Ga. S.Ct. 1985).
[2] *Illinois vs. Smith*, 464 N.E. 2d 685 (Ill. Ct. of App. 1984).
[3] *Frye vs. U.S.*, 293 F. 1013 (1923).

be. The Court ruled that, "While the Courts will go a long way in admitting expert testimony, deduced from a well-recognized scientific principle or discovery, the thing from which the deduction is made must be sufficiently established to have gained general acceptance in the particular field in which it belongs."

Although this particular case dealt narrowly with whether or not testimony about the systolic blood pressure deception test (polygraph) was acceptable as expert testimony in a court of law (it was decided that it was not), the test had been much more broadly used, in fact had been used for over 50 years, in deciding whether expert testimony in a wide range of areas would be admissible. Psychiatric and psychological testimony clearly were judged by this standard for many years. While it was never conceptualized as such, the "general acceptability standard" could easily be regarded as a "standard of care" issue; that is, general acceptability could be viewed as the level of practice of the average or relatively prudent professional, in terms of whether the assessment methodology on which the opinion was based was adequate.

Unfortunately, in actual practice, virtually all psychiatric testimony was admissible, whether or not the methodology of the evaluation conformed to generally accepted standards. In many states, Frye remains the governing standard despite being superseded in large part by a subsequent decision, *Daubert vs. Merrell Dowe*,[4] which will be discussed shortly. From the perspective of this book, however, we should regard *Frye vs. United States* as an initial step in defining an area of forensic assessment methodologies which are "generally accepted." Although it often has not been followed, the standard to be applied is that there is some consensus regarding generally accepted ways of conducting a forensic assessment.

FEDERAL RULES OF EVIDENCE

In 1975, the Federal Rules of Evidence further discussed the concept of expert testimony (Rules 702-704). An expert was defined as an individual who, by virtue of knowledge, skill, education, experience and training, was qualified to render an opinion in a particular subject area. The decision of whether or not a particular individual met those criteria was, of course, left up to the individual

---

[4] *Daubert vs. Merrell Dowe Pharmaceuticals*, 509 U.S. 579, 113 S.Ct. 2786 (1993).

judge. Once a person was so qualified, she or he could render expert opinion testimony which, in turn, was defined as being of assistance to the trier of fact and out of the range of knowledge of the ordinary layperson.

An excellent example of this would be testimony regarding the concept of Battered Spouse Syndrome. Given a scenario in which a woman has killed her abusive spouse, a lay jury or perhaps even a judge, whoever the trier of fact might be, would generally make the assumption that if the woman was being abused, she could just "get up and leave." Expert testimony regarding the concept of "learned helplessness" as part of the Battered Spouse Syndrome would assist the trier of fact and would be out of the range of knowledge of the ordinary layperson. Of course, the expert would need to be qualified in the area of assessment of Battered Spouse Syndrome.

Finally, the expert was only supposed to utilize sources of data that were "reasonably relied upon" by other experts in that same area. Here again is the implicit belief on the part of courts that there is a body of knowledge and, more important, a specific set of methodologies that should be followed by experts in any given field. In other words, the model which we proposed earlier of looking for consistencies across multiple data sources should be viewed as a procedure "reasonably relied upon" by individuals doing criminal responsibility assessments.

DAUBERT VS. MERRELL DOWE PHARMACEUTICALS

In 1993, the United States Supreme Court ruled that the Frye standard, which had been in place for 70 years, was too austere and rigid and that courts essentially should follow the Federal Rules of Evidence in determining the admissibility of expert testimony. There is a great deal of controversy regarding whether, in fact, Daubert made the criteria for admissibility of expert testimony more flexible and open or its exact opposite, more narrow and restrictive. Although the majority opinion described Frye as "austere" and sought to expand the scope of admissible expert testimony to something beyond "general acceptance," the actual criteria, upon examination, could well be seen as representing something far more narrow and restrictive than Frye. Essentially, what Daubert attempts to do is to define the concept of "reliable" in terms of known scientific principles. The individual judge in any case is regarded as a gatekeeper, and the court suggested that the following factors should be used in considering the admissability of expert testimony:

1. Whether the theory or hypothesis has been tested using some accepted scientific methodology;
2. Whether it has been subject to peer review and publication;
3. Whether the known or potential rates of error of the scientific technique justifies its use; and,
4. Whether it has achieved a degree of acceptance with the scientific community.

The court noted that these were factors to be considered and that the essential question regards scientific validity, given the specific context of the issues raised by a particular case. The court also expressed its view that "vigorous cross-examination, presentation of contrary evidence, and careful instruction on the burden of proof" were sufficient to deal with poor scientific evidence presented to a judge or jury.

The Daubert decision has caused great consternation among many individuals performing forensic mental health assessments. For instance, in a symposium presented at the biennial conference of the American Psychology Law Society in 1996, Martindale[5] noted that his practice consisted largely of child custody evaluations and questioned whether the application of these narrowly scientific criteria would help or hinder the admissibility of testimony regarding the evaluations that were being done.

One other issue, which makes the application of Daubert to forensic mental health assessments somewhat ambiguous, is a Footnote (Footnote 8) in the decision. In this Footnote, the Court states that the Federal Rules of Evidence referred to "scientific, technical, or other specialized knowledge." It then goes on to state that the current discussion, namely the analysis in Daubert, applies only to scientific knowledge, because that is what is being dealt with in the present case. The Court leaves open the question of whether or not forensic mental health assessments would fall under "scientific" or under "technical or other specialized knowledge."

Essentially, however, if one does not put too much emphasis on the error rate of the scientific technique of forensic assessment, it being well nigh impossible to determine exactly what the error rate means, in this context the other criteria, if used in a flexible manner,

---

[5] Martindale, D. *Daubert, Blackmun, Popper, and Solomon: Dealing With Daubert.* (1996, March). Paper presented as part of symposium at the Biennial Conference of the American Psychology Law Society, Hilton Head, SC.

could be very beneficial to the practice of forensic assessment within a criminal responsibility context. One could view the "accepted scientific methodology" as being the hypothesis-testing model outlined earlier, in which one looks for consistencies across multiple data sources. Clearly, criterion two has been met since this procedure has been subject to peer review and publication. Finally, the fourth criterion, that of achieving a degree of acceptance within the scientific community, is also met. Again bear in mind, that the court emphasized these were factors to be considered, not an iron-bound listing of factors that needed to be present in every case.

Looking at the model proposed earlier, then, there is an excellent argument to be made that the model followed by most serious forensic practitioners in performing a criminal responsibility assessment would meet the factors outlined in Daubert. In fact, the United States Supreme Court in Daubert eliminated the Frye rule though, to be sure, criterion number four of achieving a degree of acceptance within the scientific community appears to incorporate Frye into Daubert. The lower Federal Court of Appeals in Daubert had held that to be admitted, expert testimony had to be based on scientific principles that had gained general acceptance in the field (i.e., Frye) and this ruling was overturned by the Supreme Court. The Supreme Court, in describing Daubert as a more liberal standard, permitted admission of a much greater range of expert evidence.

In reviewing cases in which certain testimony had been admitted and other testimony not admitted, Heilbrun[6] presented a number of cases in which testimony was permitted and other cases in which testimony was not permitted under Daubert. A very interesting finding emerged: If the individual clinician follows accepted practices and does not attempt to overgeneralize from the data she or he has gathered and uses the procedure or test in the manner in which it was intended for use, then essentially the same material would be admissible under Frye or under Daubert. For example, Heilbrun in his review examines a case called *Gier vs. Educational Service Unit #16*[7] in which the Child Behavior Checklist and testimony based on it was ruled inadmissible on an issue of whether mentally retarded clients at a state school had been sexually

---

[6] Heilbrun, K. (1996, March). *Daubert and Forensic Mental Health Assessment: Use and Implication.* Paper presented at the Biennial Meeting of American Psychology Law Society, Hilton Head, SC.

[7] *Gier vs. Educational Service Unit #16*, 845 F. Supp. 1342 (D. Neb. 1994).

abused. The checklist and related testimony was ruled inadmissible under the Daubert criteria. Of course, the same testimony would have been ruled inadmissible under Frye because such testimony would certainly not reach general acceptance in the scientific community. The Child Behavior Checklist was not normed or standardized on sexually abused children and, therefore, could not be used to answer this question. In fact, such use could potentially expose the expert witness to an ethics complaint because it would be a violation of that part of the Ethics Code [Standard 202(a)] which indicates that assessment procedures should be used only for the purposes for which the instrument was originally standardized. This, in turn, reflects similar cautions in the 1985 document, *Standards for Educational and Psychological Testing.*[8] In a similar manner, Heilbrun cites several cases claimed inadmissible under Daubert, in which expert testimony was proffered to establish an "ultimate issue," namely, whether or not a particular act occurred, or whether someone possessed the kind of personality or character that would lend itself to a particular act. Testimony of both sorts would be inadmissible under Frye as well because, given that it represents a violation of ethical standards [Standards 2.01(b), 7.02(a)], such testimony would not be consistent with a standard of care defined for the practice of psychology. In *State vs. Alberico,*[9] the court ruled inadmissible testimony to demonstrate that a victim was telling the truth or to identify the perpetrator. In *Tungate vs. Commonwealth,*[10] testimony that a defendant was not a pedophile and therefore unlikely to have committed sexual abuse was ruled inadmissible. In *Steward vs. State,*[11] testimony for the prosecution about the presence of Child Sexual Abuse Syndrome was inadmissible to prove that abuse occurred. In *Isely vs. Capuchin Province,*[12] testimony regarding whether the expert believed the plaintiff that events regarding alleged sexual abuse actually occurred was ruled inadmissible. Testimony that a defendant did not fit a sex offender profile was inadmissible as a defense against a sexual assault charge.

In essence, Daubert came down on the side of the broad admission of expert testimony even when it has not achieved, in large

---

[8] American Psychological Association. (1985). *Standards for Educational and Psychological Testing.* Washington, DC: Author.
[9] *State vs. Alberico,* 861 P. 2d 192 (N.M. 1993).
[10] *Tungate vs. Commonwealth,* Ky. 901 S.W. 2d 41 (1995).
[11] *Steward vs. State,* 652 N.E. 2d 490 (Ind. 1995).
[12] *Isely vs. Capuchin Province,* 877 F. Supp. 1055 (E.D. Mich. 1995).

measure, an acceptability within the profession itself. In theory, the Daubert decision will permit the admission of a wide range of highly speculative "syndrome" mental health testimony. As noted, however, in practice much of this speculative testimony has not, in fact, been admitted. Psychologists involved in cases in which unreliable expert testimony is being presented may be called upon to help demonstrate to the judge that the proposed testimony does not meet the four factors identified by the court in Daubert.

CREDIBILITY OF THE FIELD

In the early years of expert testimony in the mental health disciplines, there was much concern about the so-called "hired gun," whose testimony would always favor the side that retained her or him. Certainly, such matters as Board certification in forensic fields have helped reduce the perception of expert witnesses as "hired guns." Imposing some standard procedures on the conduct of criminal responsibility evaluations would also assist in helping to define a standard of care in criminal forensic assessment. Whether one looks at such assessment methodology and expert testimony through the eyes of a Frye standard (generally acceptable in the field) or from a Daubert perspective (procedures generally regarded as reliable), the development of a standardized criminal responsibility evaluation format would be of great benefit to forensic psychology practitioners.

Chapter 2
ETHICAL ISSUES IN CRIMINAL RESPONSIBILITY EVALUATIONS

Many of the points discussed in Chapter 1 can be seen as having parallel reasoning in the development of ethical standards for forensic practice.

Of some interest is that, prior to the 1992 Code of Ethics of the American Psychological Association (APA),[1] there was little in the Code that specifically dealt with forensic practice. In fact, one of the problems with the 1981[2] and 1989[3] Codes was the fact that many of the difficulties and ethical pitfalls encountered by forensic practitioners were not well-defined in those Codes. It was not until the 1992 Code that there was not only a specific section (Section VII) dedicated to forensic issues, but a number of other Sections which had clear implications for forensic practice. In addition, in December of 1991, the Specialty Guidelines for Forensic Psychologists were published in the journal *Law and Human Behavior*.[4] The Specialty Guidelines provided guidance in those areas that were still somewhat vaguely defined by the APA Ethics Code. Nevertheless, the wording of several of these guidelines has been incorporated almost verbatim into the 1992 APA Ethics Code, certainly reflecting the profound influence of these Guidelines. As specialty guidelines, of course, they are not enforceable as are ethical codes but,

---

[1] American Psychological Association. (1977, March). Ethical Standards of Psychologists. *APA Monitor*, pp. 22-23.
[2] American Psychological Association. (1981). Ethical Principles of Psychologists. *American Psychologist, 36*, 633-638.
[3] American Psychological Association. (1990). Ethical Principles of Psychologists (Amended June 2, 1989). *American Psychologist, 45*, 390-395.
[4] Specialty Guidelines for Forensic Psychologists. (1991). *Law and Human Behavior, 15*(6), 655-665.

nevertheless, serve as background material that would help someone more fully define the various parts of the Ethics Code.

Let us now turn to a consideration of these specific issues.

ETHICAL PRINCIPLES OF PSYCHOLOGISTS AND CODE OF CONDUCT

The 1992 version of the Ethics Code was initially published in
the *American Psychologist* in December of 1992. From its general
principles on through the specific ethical standards, one can see very
clearly the application of this Code in the practice of criminal responsibility assessments. For instance, General Principle A - Competence, speaks of psychologists "recognizing the boundaries of their
particular competencies and the limits of their expertise." There is
always a temptation, within a forensic setting, to "overrepresent
oneself" in terms of one's expertise due to the very nature of the
adversarial judicial system. The Principle goes on to state that "they
[i.e., psychologists] provide only those services and use only those
techniques for which they are qualified by education, training and
experience." Note how closely this tracks the definition of expert
under the Federal Rules of Evidence. In Principle B - Integrity, and
in Principle C - Professional and Scientific Responsibility, the idea
of avoiding improper and potentially harmful dual relationships is
clearly stated, exhorting the psychologist to "clarify professional
roles and obligations." So very often in forensic settings, role boundaries become blurred between therapist and forensic examiner and
between fact and expert witness. While these general principles are
not enforceable under the Ethics Code, they do serve to alert psychologists to these potential areas of difficulty. Finally, as another
example, in Principle F - Social Responsibility, there is a statement
that, "Psychologists try to avoid misuse of their work." This is an
ongoing ethical dilemma in forensic practice since adversarial attorneys will attempt to use psychological data for the furtherance of
their cases and psychologists are constantly in a quandary regarding
the appropriate release of certain materials.

Moving to the general standards, early on, Standard 1.02 - The
Relationship of Ethics and Law, talks about the conflict at times
between the ethical responsibilities and law. While there is a clear
recognition of this potential conflict area, there is a very strong statement that "the psychologist must make known her or his commitment to the Ethics Code." In actual practice, what this means is if,

for instance, a subpoena is received demanding the disclosure of certain data which the psychologist feels would be harmful to the client, the psychologist must not have a "knee jerk" response to the subpoena, but rather write to the individual who has issued the subpoena and note the areas of conflict with the Ethics Code (see Appendix A on pp. 63-65 for format). If this cannot be resolved in this informal manner, the psychologist needs to file a motion to quash or a motion for a protective order (see Appendix B on pp. 67-71 for format). This will, at the very least, trigger a review (usually in-camera) by the judge who will rule on whether or not the material needs to be released. The important way of complying with the Ethics Code is to make the opposition to the subpoena and the reasons for that opposition well-known. If the judge ultimately orders that the material needs to be released, then it can be, for there is no ethical violation in following a lawful court order.

Standard 1.03 - Professional and Scientific Relationships. This standard addresses the fact that psychological services are performed only in the context of a defined professional or scientific relationship or role, and the forensic section of the Code is cross-referenced. Once again, as part of our unfortunate history as an evolving discipline, forensic practitioners became involved in giving "off-the-cuff" analyses of certain individuals whom they had not examined. This part of the Code strongly urges us not to do this.

Standard 1.04 - Boundaries of Competence. In addition to dealing with the issues mentioned previously concerning the parallel nature of this Section and the Federal Rules of Evidence regarding the definition of an expert, this standard speaks of taking reasonable steps to assure the competence of work in areas which have not yet been well-defined and which are emerging. An example is the controversy regarding repressed memories. Someone presenting expert testimony in such an area would need to acknowledge the controversies in the field and carefully present only testimony that has a recognized scientific basis, and to concede limitations regarding validity and reliability.

Standard 1.07, Describing the Nature and Results of Psychological Services, speaks of providing "appropriate information beforehand about the nature of such services and appropriate information later about results and conclusions." This goes to the whole issue of informed consent in forensic evaluations, especially criminal responsibility evaluations. The need in a criminal responsibility evaluation to inform the defendant of the nature of the evaluation, the lack of confidentiality in the evaluation and to whom the results of the evaluation will be revealed, are all important aspects of the informed consent to the evaluative process. Although it is beyond the scope of this practice manual to discuss the variations seen in this matter by various states, suffice it to say that there are some states in which, if an expert is retained by a defense attorney and reaches a conclusion that is not helpful to that defense attorney, the negative opinion is shielded by attorney-client privilege and need not be revealed to the government (e.g., *United States vs. Alvarez,* 1975;[5] *State vs. Pratt,* 1979[6]). On the other hand, several states have ruled that, once a psychiatric issue is raised, the defendant has in essence waived attorney-client privilege and the results of the evaluation are available to the government (*Edney vs. State;*[7] *Noggle vs. Marshall*[8]). If the expert has been retained by the government, on the other hand, then any material that would be of assistance to the defense must be revealed. Finally, if the evaluation is Court-ordered, no privilege at all exists and the results of the evaluation need to be turned over to all concerned parties (i.e., to the judge, to the defense attorney and to the government's attorney). Clearly, then, this is a complex issue and the clinician doing a forensic assessment must know the law in the state or Federal jurisdiction in which she or he is practicing. Once the evaluator knows the law, it can be incorporated into an appropriate informed consent document. For instance, the defendant being examined by an expert retained by the defense in a state in which the attorney-client privilege doctrine prevails, would be told something along the following lines: "You need to be aware of the fact that, unlike the traditional doctor-patient relationship in which what you would tell me is confidential, I will be sharing the results of this evaluation with your defense attorney. This will not go beyond your attorney unless you and your attorney choose to use it in court. Under those circumstances, the report will be revealed to the government."

On the other hand, if one is working in a state in which there is disclosure to the government, one would state to the defendant, in addition to the nonconfidential nature of the relationship, "I am here to conduct an evaluation at the request of your defense attorney. Once this evaluation is complete, it will be revealed to both your attorney and to the District Attorney."

---

[5] *U.S. vs. Alvarez,* 519 F. 2d 1036 (3rd Circuit 1975).
[6] *State vs. Pratt,* 398 N.E. 2d 421 (Md. Ct. App. 1979).
[7] *Edney vs. State,* 556 F. 2d 556 (2nd Circuit 1977).
[8] *Noggle vs. Marshall,* 706 F. 2d 1408 (6th Circuit 1983).

If you are retained by the prosecution, the informed consent statement would be, again, along the lines that the evaluation is not confidential, that you have been retained by the government and that the results of the evaluation will be provided to the government attorney and to the defense attorney.

Finally, if the evaluation is Court-ordered, the defendant must be informed of that fact and also of the fact that the report will be revealed to all parties involved, namely, the judge, the defense attorney and the prosecutor or District Attorney.

Clearly, there also needs to be an assessment of the defendant's competency to render informed consent. In the absence of a Court-ordered evaluation in which, technically, consent is not required (though even here it would be advisable), any evaluation on behalf of either a defense attorney or a prosecutor demands that the defendant be competent to render an informed consent to the procedure. If such consent cannot be obtained, then the evaluation should under no circumstances proceed. A defense attorney can, of course, give substitute judgment for the conduct of the evaluation but a District Attorney or prosecutor cannot. Under such circumstances, the defendant's incompetence to render informed consent to the evaluation needs to be made known to the court. One additional point is of importance here, namely, that incompetence to render informed consent does not necessarily refer to incompetence to participate in other decisions or to be not criminally responsible. Each of these functional capacities (see Grisso, 1986[9]) must be examined in its own right. Grisso has discussed, quite extensively, this concept of functional legal capacities, cautioning that they cannot be inferred directly from clinical assessments. This direct inference procedure is one of the most common errors made by practitioners making the transition from a traditional clinical to a forensic practice. In addition, Grisso outlines in a very comprehensive manner the reasons for regarding each functional capacity as unique and distinct from the others. For instance, someone who is found incompetent to stand trial may very well be competent to participate in or reject a particular form of treatment. Someone who is competent to stand trial may not be competent to represent herself or himself or waive counsel.

The question has often arisen whether written informed consent is essential. Although this is certainly an ideal, many defendants are

---

[9] Grisso, T. (1986). *Evaluating Competencies.* New York: Plenum.

too paranoid to sign such a document. In such cases, the discussion of the consent issues should be included in the body of the final report, including observation of the reasons why the examiner feels that the defendant was competent to give the informed consent, despite the refusal to sign the form (see Appendix C on pp. 73-78 for suggested formats).

Rendering such informed consent is not only good forensic practice but several recent court decisions have been critical of mental health professionals who do not provide such informed consent to the defendants whom they have examined. For example, in *Department of Youth Services vs. A Juvenile* (1986),[10] the court ruled that it was reversible error to permit testimony by a psychiatrist who had interviewed a juvenile because the doctor had failed to warn the youth in advance that their conversations were not confidential and could be used against him in a commitment extension proceeding. Even though no actual communications from the juvenile were disclosed at trial, the doctor rendered a diagnosis based partially on conversations with the youth that were not preceded by any warnings. A new trial was awarded by the court based on "a substantial risk of a miscarriage of justice."

Standard 1.16 - Misuse of Psychologist's Work. As noted earlier, a psychologist should not participate in an activity in which her or his skills or data may be misused but, more importantly, if a psychologist learns of misuse or misrepresentation of that work, she or he should take reasonable steps to correct or minimize the misuse or misrepresentation. This can clearly become problematic in the performance of a criminal responsibility assessment. That is, one is performing an evaluation most often at the request of a particular attorney. If one finds out that that attorney is misusing the data, clearly, one cannot reveal this to opposing counsel because of issues of attorney-client privilege. Contracting with that attorney to provide services (i.e., an evaluation) places the psychologist under the rubric of attorney-client privilege, making the data and opinion "work product." On the other hand, this ethical principle should alert the psychologist to the fact that the attorney who has misrepresented her or him may well need to be contacted in order to bring to the attorney's attention the inappropriate use of the data. Obviously, documentation of this contact should be maintained within the psychologist's files. Informally, this may serve to put the attorney

---

[10] *Department of Youth Services vs. A Juvenile*, 499 N.E. 2d 812 (Mass. Sup. Jud. Ct. 1986).

on notice that the psychologist, if testifying, may qualify certain conclusions that will make evident the attempted misuse of the data. Under such circumstances, it is unlikely that the attorney will call that psychologist as a witness.

Standard 1.17 - Multiple Relationships. This Section of the Ethics Code deals with the necessity of psychologists to be sensitive to the potentially harmful effects of other contacts on their work and on the persons with whom they deal. It suggests avoiding a multiple relationship if "it appears likely that such a relationship reasonably might impair the psychologist's objectivity or otherwise interfere with the psychologist effectively performing his or her functions as a psychologist or might harm or exploit the other party." Generally, while most clinicians can understand the reasons for this in a clinical setting, this principle has been poorly understood within the forensic domain. The important point to be made is that one cannot be an effective therapist in terms of helping the patient deal with her or his difficulty if one has also been involved in doing a comprehensive forensic evaluation of that individual. In other words, if one has done a comprehensive assessment, interviewed many witnesses, reviewed many reports, assessed the possibilities of malingering or secondary gain, then one in a sense "knows too much" to be of assistance to the patient and to maintain the free-floating attention that is necessary to truly help the patient unravel her or his personal difficulties. The therapist also should make every effort to avoid becoming involved in any litigation as an expert witness. Therapists frequently feel that, because they know the patient so well, they can answer relevant legal questions. However, given the comprehensive model of forensic assessment noted earlier, it is virtually impossible to address these issues because psychotherapy is not directed toward issues such as obtaining external verification of the patient's perceptions. If the therapist does become involved in litigation, she or he must scrupulously avoid rendering any opinions relevant to the legal matters at hand but rather simply describe what the course of the psychotherapy was and how the patient may have changed. Thus, the treating therapist is essentially testifying as a lay witness, not as an expert witness. This is a crucial distinction that many attorneys fail to recognize. Attorneys customarily refer a patient to a physician for examination and treatment if deemed necessary. Indeed, when the examination is solely for the purpose of diagnosis in order to render appropriate treatment, the mixing of roles is permissible, though it is rare that an attorney will *not* expect some expert opinion in the future. Forensic psychologists and psychiatrists need to inform attorneys, however, that a diagnosis made as part of a treatment program is not the same as rendering an expert opinion in a legal proceeding and that a treating therapist should never be called as an expert witness. A recent article in *Professional Psychology* by Greenberg and Shuman[11] comprehensively outlines these role differences (see Table 1 on page 17).

Standard 1.21 - Third Party Requests for Services. When a psychologist agrees to provide services at the request of a third party, for instance an attorney, there must be at the outset of the service a clarification of the nature of the relationship with each party such that the defendant does not come to perceive the psychologist as a therapist. This in part has been described earlier in the Informed Consent Section. If a foreseeable risk arises of the psychologist being called upon to perform conflicting roles, there must be a clarification of the nature and direction of responsibilities.

Standard 1.23 - Documentation of Professional and Scientific Work. Section B of this Standard is directly related to the Specialty Guidelines for Forensic Psychologists. This refers to the fact that when there is a reasonable anticipation on the part of the psychologist that the records of their professional services may be used in a legal proceeding, "they have a responsibility to create and maintain documentation in the kind of detail and quality that would be consistent with reasonable scrutiny in an adjudicative form." Of course this would be the ideal for all documentation and recordkeeping but, especially when it may be reviewed by a court, by attorneys or by opposing expert witnesses, the documentation must be quite extensive and the nature of the derivation of the conclusions from the data very clearly specified.

Standard 2.01, Section (b), dealing with evaluation, diagnosis and intervention in a professional context, is especially relevant to criminal responsibility assessments. It is also a critically important part of the Ethics Code because earlier codes had no section that specifically dealt with having adequate data on which to base one's conclusions. In the past, this left ethics committees in some kind of quandary because the closest they were able to come to an ethical violation would be to state that a person misused certain assessment devices. This Section is highly responsive to needs within a forensic context, specifically one in which a criminal responsibility evalu-

---

[11] Greenberg, S., & Shuman, D. (1997). Irreconcilable Conflict Between Therapeutic and Forensic Roles. *Journal of Professional Psychology: Research and Practice, 28*(1), 50-57.

TABLE 1: IRRECONCILABLE DIFFERENCES BETWEEN THERAPEUTIC CARE AND FORENSIC EXAMINATION RELATIONSHIPS*

	Therapeutic Care	Forensic Examination	Type of Conflict
1. Whose client is patient/litigant?	The mental health practitioner	The attorney's	Professional Role
2. The relational privilege that governs disclosure in each relationship	Therapist-patient privilege	Attorney-client and attorney work-product privilege	Professional Role
3. The cognitive set and evaluative attitude of each expert	Supportive, accepting, empathic	Neutral, objective, detached	Professional Role
4. The nature and degree of alliance in each relationship	A helping relationship, allies; rarely adversarial	An evaluative relationship; frequently adversarial	Professional Role
5. The differing areas of competency of each expert	Therapy techniques for treatment of the impairment	Forensic examination techniques relevant to the legal claim	Adequacy of Foundation
6. The nature of the hypotheses tested by each expert	Diagnostic criteria for the purpose of therapy	Psychological criteria for purpose of legal adjudication	Adequacy of Foundation
7. The amount and control of structure in each relationship	Patient-structured and relatively less structured than forensic examination	Examiner-structured and relatively more structured than therapy	Adequacy of Foundation
8. The scrutiny applied to the information used in the process, and the role of historical truth	Mostly based on information from the person being treated, with little external scrutiny of that information by the therapist	Litigant information supplemented with and verified by collateral sources and scrutinized by the examiner, adversaries and the court	Adequacy of Foundation
9. The goal of the professional in each relationship	Therapist attempts to benefit the patient by working within the therapeutic relationship	Examiner advocates for the results and implications of the evaluation for the benefit of the court	Professional Role
10. The impact on each relationship of critical judgment by the psychologist	The basis of the relationship is the therapeutic alliance and critical judgment is likely to impair that alliance	The basis of the relationship is evaluative and critical judgment is less likely to cause serious emotional harm	Professional Role

*Note. From "Irreconcilable Conflict Between Therapeutic and Forensic Roles," by S. Greenberg and D. Shuman, 1997, *Journal of Professional Psychology: Research and Practice, 28*(1), pp. 50-57. Copyright 1997 by American Psychological Association. Adapted with permission.

ation is being done, and again refers back by implication to the standard of care discussed previously, namely that the information and techniques are "sufficient to provide appropriate substantiation for findings." If a psychologist were to reach an opinion in a criminal responsibility evaluation based only on the clinical interview and had not used the multiple sources of data described earlier, then one could clearly state that there was a violation of Standard 2.01, Section (b) due to the insufficient information relied upon. This would also provide excellent ammunition for cross-examination of that expert.

Standard 2.02 - Competence and Appropriate Use of Assessments and Interventions. Section A refers to the use of assessment techniques, interviews, tests or instruments "in a manner and for purposes that are appropriate in light of the research on or evidence of the usefulness and proper application of the techniques." It is unfortunately an all too common phenomenon that psychologists will make "wild" interpretations of certain psychological tests or utilize tests in criminal responsibility settings for purposes for which the tests have not been validated or for norm groups on whom the test has not been normed or standardized. This can clearly lead not only to frank distortions but misapplication and misunderstanding of the significance of a test score.

An example of such a distortion would be the testimony of a psychologist who described the Minnesota Multiphasic Personality Inventory as "an emotional x-ray" and further stated that the test could reveal what was going on in the defendant's mind at the time of the offense.

In addition, Standard 2.02, Section (b) speaks about avoiding the misuse of assessment techniques and taking reasonable steps to "prevent others from misusing the information, including refraining from releasing raw test results or raw data to persons other than to patients or clients as appropriate who are not qualified to use such information." Again, this is a dramatic improvement over the earlier Ethics Codes which really did not address this point at all. Of some interest is that this issue was discussed in the *General Guidelines for Providers of Psychological Services* (1987).[12] Generally, psychologists have recognized the conflict and have attempted to resolve it by inviting the party demanding the records to provide the

---

[12] American Psychological Association. (1987). *General Guidelines for Providers of Psychological Services.* Washington, DC: Author.

name of the licensed professional competent to interpret the data to the holder of the records and then either send the records to that licensed professional or arrange a meeting where the records are mutually reviewed. Generally, this informal approach is successful and most often an attorney who has issued a subpoena will merely provide the name of the licensed psychologist who has been retained to review the records.

If counsel persists in demanding the records, and will not provide the name of the opposing expert, it is then the clinician's responsibility to file a motion to quash the subpoena or to seek a protective order. Once this is done, the court will review the matter and the judge will issue an opinion detailing whether or not the psychologist is obligated to reveal the records to opposing counsel. As noted before, as long as the attempt to adhere to the ethical code is documented, following a lawful court order would in no way be regarded as a violation of the Ethics Code.

In some instances, because of the specific rules of discovery, an attorney might not be willing to disclose the name of the expert who has been retained. A suggested alternative format under these circumstances is to write to the attorney who has issued the subpoena and obtain a notarized statement that the records will be revealed only to the psychologist retained and will not be disclosed to anyone else.

A suggested format for responding to the initial request for raw data follows below:

> Re: subpoena to (doctor) in the case of (client)

Dear (attorney):

> This responds to your letter of (date) requesting that I comply with a subpoena issued from (court).

> That subpoena requests the production of the results of psychological tests conducted on (date). The *Ethical Principles of Psychologists and Code of Conduct* (APA, 1992) prohibit me from sending you that test data.

> If you will consider providing me the name of the licensed psychologist qualified to interpret the data whom you have retained to review the material, I will be glad to provide the data directly to that psychologist.

> Very truly yours,

It is important that the clinician utilize this approach for a variety of reasons. First, of course, is that the ethical standards prohibit the disclosure. Second, the courts have essentially recognized the legitimacy of the demand to reveal raw data only to another licensed psychologist. The courts, according to several recent decisions, do not recognize other grounds for withholding test data. For instance, in *Massachusetts vs. Trapp* (1985),[13] the Court ruled that there was no violation of the defendant's right against self-incrimination in providing the state with results of "non-testimonial scientific tests," including the raw data from psychological tests. The defendant in this case argued the withholding of the data on the wrong grounds, namely of violation of Fifth Amendment privilege, rather than on the ethical principles noted previously.

Standard 3.02 - Statements by Others. This Standard urges psychologists to make reasonable efforts to prevent others from making deceptive statements about the psychologist's practice, professional or scientific activities. The statement recognizes that these are frequently out of the psychologist's control but, nevertheless, reasonable efforts need to be taken. For example, in a recent case, a psychologist was retained to provide expertise regarding the fact that individuals who batter spouses do not necessarily murder them. The opening statement by the defense attorney misrepresented the nature of the opinion and indicated that this psychologist would give testimony that the defendant did not "fit the profile of a murderer." Not only would this be an inaccurate statement, it would also violate several of the Ethical Standards already discussed regarding proper use of assessment instruments and not making statements out of the bounds of one's competence. The psychologist probably notified the attorney that that was an improper and inappropriate characterization of the testimony. The attorney did not subsequently utilize this psychologist's testimony.

Standard 7.01 - Professionalism. This Standard represents the beginning of the forensic section of the 1992 Ethics Code. It restates many of the earlier principles specifically in light of the forensic context, such as basing forensic work "on appropriate knowledge of and competence in the areas underlying such work." For example, a psychologist who observes that, in a particular criminal responsibility assessment, the matter of organic impairment may be quite important, would not undertake to perform a comprehen-

---

[13] *Massachusetts vs. Trapp,* 485 N.E. 2d 162 (Mass. Sup. Jud. Ct. 1985).

sive neuropsychological assessment unless she or he had been properly trained in this kind of evaluation. In fact, several recent cases have laid the precedent for such specialized knowledge in expert testimony. In Frederick,[14] a case was reversed on appeal because the trial court had failed to appoint an expert with specific experience in Multiple Personality Disorder (MPD). A similar reversal occurred in Doe[15] due to the failure to appoint an expert in Battered Spouse Syndrome and Posttraumatic Stress Disorder. Finally, in McLane,[16] the reversal occurred due to failure to appoint an expert on brain-behavior relationships.

Standard 7.02, Section A restates the very important Standard 2.01, Section (b) having to do with the basing of recommendations on techniques sufficient to provide appropriate substantiation for the findings. An important issue here is that the individual about whom conclusions are being rendered needs to be personally interviewed. One, in fact, cannot provide written or oral forensic reports or testimony about the psychological characteristics of an individual in most circumstances unless the psychologist has conducted an examination of the individual adequate to support the statements or conclusions. The proper application of this ethical standard should serve to put the curbs on certain professionals who misuse what is called "behavioral science profiling." These techniques, well-documented in many publications from the Behavioral Sciences Unit of the Federal Bureau of Investigation, are utilized to identify *classes* of individuals, rather than specific people. Several psychologists have, in fact, misused this behavioral science profiling in order to suggest that a given individual is the perpetrator of a particular crime, based on an analysis of the crime scene and certain supporting documentation, without ever having seen the individual.

Standard 7.02, Section C recognizes that in certain forensic contexts, especially in the criminal responsibility area, an attorney may wish to block the examination for various legal reasons. This section states that "When, despite reasonable efforts, such an examination (i.e., a personal interview of the individual) is not feasible, psychologists clarify the impact of their limited information on the reliability and validity of their reports and testimony and they approximately limit the nature and extent of their conclusions or rec-

---

[14] *Frederick vs. Oklahoma,* 902 P. 2d 1092 (Ok. Crim. App. 1995).

[15] *Doe vs. Sup. Ct. of L.A. Cty.,* 45 Cal. Rptr. 2d 288 (1995).

[16] *N.Y. vs. McLane,* 631 NYS 2d 976.

ommendations." In other words, in practical terms, an attorney may refuse to make a particular defendant available for interview. Under those circumstances, no conclusion regarding that person's mental state can be made. On other occasions, certain witnesses, family or friends may either refuse to be interviewed or may be informed by the attorney not to participate in the evaluation. Under these circumstances, the Ethical Code is very clear: The conclusions need to be qualified in light of the missing data. An example follows:

> Mr. L* was charged with a sexual assault on a woman who, in the police report, stated that the defendant was "talking out of his head." Mr. L, in fact, had a lengthy history of psychiatric hospitalizations and at the time of the offense was on a weekend pass from a psychiatric facility. The psychologist who, in this case, had been retained by the defense counsel sought to interview the complaining witness to ascertain the meaning of "he was talking out of his head" which could clearly be relevant to the mental state of the defendant at the time of the offense. Based on the government's refusal to provide this witness, the conclusion of the report stated that no definitive opinion on criminal responsibility could be reached since the complaining witness was not made available for interview. However, the report did note that progress notes from the hospital prior to the defendant's weekend pass and psychiatric consultations from the jail following his arrest revealed an active and overt psychosis.

Standard 7.03 - Clarification of Role, essentially restates Standard 1.17 and 1.21, again within a forensic context.

SPECIALTY GUIDELINES FOR FORENSIC PSYCHOLOGISTS

As noted earlier, these guidelines, although informed by the APA Ethics Code, are "designed to provide more specific guidance to forensic psychologists in monitoring their professional conduct when acting in assistance to courts, parties to legal proceedings, correctional and forensic mental health facilities, and legislative agencies." As noted before, because these are guidelines, they are "an aspirational model of desirable professional practice," and are not, therefore, enforceable by an ethics committee. They, neverthe-

---

* All cases cited in this text are matters of public record. The reports are part of the court record. Nevertheless, names, dates and places have been disguised to whatever extent feasible without losing the essence of the case.

less, serve as background data which will help to expand an ethics committee's understanding of certain forensic issues. One important issue is that the guidelines are to be used by individuals who are "engaged regularly as experts and represent themselves as such." Clearly, someone regularly engaged in performing criminal responsibility assessments should be familiar with these guidelines. The guidelines do not contradict anything in the *Ethical Principles of Psychologists* and Code of Conduct, but rather amplify them in the context of the practice of forensic psychology.

As an example of this concept of amplifying upon the APA Code of Ethics, we may note Guideline III. Although III-A essentially tracks the Ethics Code (and the Federal Rules of Evidence) by talking about practicing only in areas of psychology in which the psychologist has "specialized knowledge, skill, education and experience," the Guidelines go further. For instance, in Part B of Guideline III, it puts on the shoulders of the psychologist an affirmative obligation to "present to the court regarding the specific matters to which they will testify, the boundaries of their competence, the factual bases (knowledge, skill, experience, training and education) for their qualification as an expert and the relevance of those factual bases to their qualifications as an expert on the specific matters at issue." In other words, if an expert has performed a criminal responsibility evaluation, she or he needs not only to demonstrate training in reference to this but must also be able to relate the specific training to the specific issues at hand in a particular case. Practicing within the bounds of one's competence is also further broken down within the same Principle to understanding the legal and professional standards, understanding the civil rights of the individuals involved in the legal proceedings and recognizing when personal values, moral beliefs or personal and professional relationships may interfere with one's ability to practice.

In a similar manner, Section IV, Relationships, specifies, in addition to the above-noted areas of competency and relationships that might interfere with an objective and competent job, "the known scientific bases and limitations of the methods and procedures that they employ and their qualifications to employ such methods and procedures." This, again, is an affirmative obligation and places on the psychologist within this setting not only the need to be qualified to utilize certain procedures, but also to be aware enough of the research and related ethical issues such that one can inform an attorney whether or not expert testimony in a particular area can even be given. To amplify on the example presented previously, if an attorney asks a psychologist to render an opinion on whether a particular defendant "fits the profile" of, for instance, a rapist or a murderer, the psychologist has an obligation to inform the attorney that such profiles do not exist, that there is no research basis to render a conclusion in such matters and that, in fact, it would be unethical to do so.

Section IV-D amplifies on Ethical Standard 1.17, Multiple Relationships, within the forensic context. Section IV-E, again, expands on the Ethics Code's description of Informed Consent, but also highlights the very important issue that, once the informed consent is given, "The psychologist may not use the evaluation work product for other purposes without explicit waiver to do so by the client or the client's legal representative." For instance, if a psychologist is retained to perform a criminal responsibility evaluation, that psychologist should under no circumstances allow, either personally or by someone else, use of the data to address another legal issue (e.g., an assessment of future violent behavior). This would require a totally separate and distinct assessment.

Section V, dealing with Confidentiality and Privilege, again provides more depth and more detail to the need outlined in the Ethics Code to explain limitations upon confidentiality.

SECTION VI - METHODS AND PROCEDURES

As noted earlier, Guideline VI-B is incorporated into the Ethics Code itself, and is about providing especially well-documented records when it can be anticipated that legal proceedings will be forthcoming. Principle VI-B states that when psychologists have "foreknowledge that their professional services will be used in an adjudicative forum, they incur a special responsibility to provide the best documentation possible under the circumstances."

As a corollary to the model proposed earlier of hypothesis testing and consistency across multiple data sources for criminal responsibility evaluations, Section VI-C states, "The forensic psychologist maintains professional integrity by examining the issue at hand from all reasonable perspectives, actively seeking information that will differentially test plausible rival hypotheses."

Principle VI-E urges some degree of caution in utilizing the multiple data sources. Recognizing that these are necessary in the completion of a criminal responsibility evaluation as well as in other forensic evaluations, the principle states, "When forensic psychologists seek data from third parties, prior records, or other sources, they do so only with the prior approval of the relevant legal party or as a consequence of an order of a court to conduct the forensic evaluation." Clearly, then, one does not seek such third party information without the knowledge of the client or the client's legal representative, unless the evaluation is being conducted under Court order. When gathering third party data, "the origins of those data are clarified in any professional product." In addition, there is a special responsibility to ensure that the data, if relied upon, "were gathered in a manner standard for the profession." This, once again, tracks the Federal Rules of Evidence, which talks about the type of evidence "reasonably relied upon" by other experts in the same field, again referring to certain accepted manners of data collection and again highlighting the necessity of gathering the data in some standardized uniform fashion.

A very important point is discussed in Section VI-G, which is specifically applicable to defendants raising a mental state defense, such as insanity or lack of criminal responsibility. Federal Rule of Procedure 12.2(c) must be followed by forensic psychologists in performing criminal responsibility evaluations. Essentially, statements made by a defendant in the course of a forensic examination can be admitted into evidence only on an issue respecting mental condition on which the defendant has introduced testimony. In other words, if a psychologist conducting a criminal responsibility evaluation is informed by the defendant that, in addition to the crime for which an insanity defense is being raised, the defendant has also committed other crimes, that information would not be admissible. Similarly inadmissible would be "any other fruits of the statement." Because of the fact that forensic psychologists are often not in a position to know "what evidence, documentation or element of a written product may be or may lend to a fruit of the statement, they exercise extreme caution in preparing reports or offering testimony prior to the defendant's assertion of a mental state claim or the defendant's introduction of testimony regarding a mental condition."

Section VI-H provides the basis for Ethical Standards 7.02 B and C, referring only to writing reports or testifying about individuals whom they have personally examined, and when it was impossible to do an examination, clarifying the impact of the limitations on the reliability and validity of their report or testimony.

Section VII, which deals with public and professional communications, again provides more details to the ethical principle dealing with correcting misuse or misrepresentation of one's testimony. When disagreements with an opposing expert arise, these must be presented in a fair and accurate manner, dealing with the data, theories, standards and opinions of the other expert or party, rather than in any personal confrontations or statements about the opposing expert. An important distinction is drawn between gathering data in a fair and objective manner and forcefully representing the data and reasoning upon which a conclusion is based. The most important aspect of this section is that the psychologist must avoid any attempt "to engage in partisan distortion or misrepresentation." Either by commission or omission, they must not participate in a misrepresentation of their own evidence, nor should they try to "avoid, deny or subvert" contrary evidence. As noted earlier, this can become and often represents a conflict between the Ethics Code of a psychologist who is bound to present all sides of a picture objectively and fairly and the ethical code of an attorney who is bound to present the most forceful case for her or his client. An attorney may feel, for instance, the need to avoid, eliminate or limit certain aspects of the psychologist's report or testimony. The psychologist, while respecting the attorney's need to do so, must not, according to this guideline, participate in that attempt.

The "Ultimate Issue" Issue

In recent years, the issue of whether or not mental health professionals should address so-called ultimate legal issues* has been receiving a great deal of attention. Few psychologists would dispute the fact that, in one's report, one should not state that a patient is or is not sane or does or does not have "diminished capacity," for these are *exclusively legal issues.* However, the difficulty arises when one goes to the level of behavioral description just below these issues. There are many who contend that even addressing the criteria for these issues (sometimes described as penultimate) is going beyond the bounds of our expertise and there are some who regard such statements as actually unethical. Some scholars have pointed out or suggested that mental health professionals involved in forensic issues should do no more than describe the human behavior which has been observed, leaving such issues as whether or not the defendant "lacked substantial capacity" to the trier of fact.

---

* The actual legal question, that is, is a given individual competent or incompetent to stand trial; criminally responsible or not responsible (by reason of mental disease or defect) for a particular criminal act.

The contention in this book will be that such a position is flawed for two reasons. First, if one has done and performed a careful and comprehensive forensic evaluation, with all of the empirical referents needed, in a description of behavior it becomes little more than a semantic point to describe that behavior in a great deal of detail or to state that the behavior constituted "a lack of substantial capacity to appreciate wrongfulness." In other words, if, as the scholars and commentators have pointed out, one describes a situation in which an individual is grossly psychotic, misperceives an individual walking down the street toward him as the devil because "the devil always wears a red tie" and subsequently assaults that individual, is there really a difference between describing that behavior, and talking about the gross impairment of reality testing (a clinical issue) and then subsequently stating, "the patient, therefore, lacked substantial capacity to appreciate the wrongfulness of his behavior" due to the severity of his psychotic distortions?

While this may be merely a semantic issue, the more troubling issue is what actually happens in a court of law when a mental health professional refuses to address an ultimate issue, stating that it is either unethical to do so or going beyond the bounds of one's competence to do so. What, unfortunately, happens is that courts will turn to less well-trained, less competent, less ethical individuals who will be glad to give an opinion on any topic without adequate empirical verification. A rather chilling example of this occurred several years ago in the state of Texas. Most readers are, no doubt, aware of the case, *Barefoot vs. Estelle*.[17] In that case, an opinion was rendered by a psychiatrist that he could tell that a given defendant would pose a threat of future violence to society without even examining that individual and that he could render that opinion with "100% certainty." If one considers for a moment the hypothetical situation where one of us refuses to comment on an ultimate issue and a mental health professional, such as the one in this case, is willing to do so without even examining the individual, it is clear that the court will pay attention to that professional willing to give an opinion. This does not suggest that we should respond in kind, giving opinions without adequate empirical basis. Rather, I would contend that in the best of all possible worlds perhaps mental health professionals may not have to address ultimate legal issues. This should be made clear to courts, to attorneys and to various judicial

---

[17] *Barefoot vs. Estelle*, 51 U.S.L.W. 5189 (U.S. S.Ct. 7/6/83).

bodies through a process of ongoing continuing education. In the short run, however, to prevent the kinds of abuses noted earlier, we may very well need to address ultimate issues but be sure we are doing so by providing ample empirical bases for our opinions.

Chapter 3
HISTORICAL OVERVIEW AND CURRENT STATE OF THE LAW

While an in-depth historical background of the insanity defense is beyond the scope of this manual, a brief overview would be of some assistance in understanding and putting into context some of the issues that the forensic practitioner needs to address in doing a criminal responsibility evaluation.

The first case that is of relevance to our consideration is the case of Daniel McNaughten in England in 1843.[1] McNaughten was an individual who developed a delusional system concerning the government of Queen Victoria. He shot one of the lesser Ministers in Queen Victoria's cabinet. It became obvious to people who talked with McNaughten that he was quite delusional. In the aftermath of this case, there emerged the so-called McNaughten or right-wrong test. It consisted of two sections. First, it spoke about an individual being so mentally ill that he or she did not know the nature and quality of his or her act - that is, a person who did not really know exactly what the act itself was. The example was given of an individual who strangled someone but who did not think he was strangling somebody but rather thought that he was merely squeezing a lemon. Such an individual did not "appreciate the nature and quality of the act." Another example given was of a mentally retarded individual who thought that it would be amusing to decapitate someone because he thought it would be funny to watch the person get up in the morning and look for his head. He obviously did not understand the quality of the act, namely that decapitation caused death.

---

[1] *Daniel McNaughten's Case*, 10 Cl. & Fin. 200 8 Eng. Rep. 718 (1843).

The second part of the McNaughten standard asked whether, even if a person knew the nature and quality of the act, that individual was incapable by virtue of a mental illness of knowing that what she or he was doing was wrong. Especially in recent years, the McNaughten standard has come under tremendous criticism by people who regard it as an exclusively cognitive test (knowledge of right and wrong) and does not take into account the complexity of human beings.

The second major development in thinking regarding criminal responsibility emerged in the form of the so-called irresistible impulse test: The defendant lacked the willpower to control his or her behavior.[2] Most frequently this test is used along with the McNaughten standard, rather than standing by itself as a criterion used to decide the issue of criminal responsibility. The test for criminal responsibility then becomes an "either/or" situation. In other words, if an individual had a mental disorder, she or he could be exculpated for criminal activity if (a) she or he could not understand the nature and quality of the act; or (b) she or he did not know that the act was wrong; or (c) she or he was irresistibly impelled to commit the act. The problem, of course, was the inability to define how strong an impulse had to be before it was irresistible. What, for instance, would be the difference between an irresistible impulse and an unresisted impulse, one which an individual could not control and one which an individual chose not to control? Despite attempts by some jurisdictions to define irresistible impulse as "the policeman at the elbow," this test did not appear to attract a substantial following. Many mental health professionals stated that the definitions given were too restrictive and that cognition alone was far too narrow a basis on which to state an opinion regarding a person's mental state at the time of the offense. In 1954, the courts responded with the so-called product test, named after Durham,[3] the defendant in the particular case. The Durham test stated that an accused was not criminally responsible if the criminal activity was the product of the mental disease or defect. The test was designed to give "the widest possible scope to expert evaluation and expert testimony." The Durham standard was not without its own set of problems and predicaments, however. There were two major stumbling

---

[2] *Davis vs. U.S.,* 165 U.S. 373, 378 (1897).
[3] *Durham vs. U.S.,* 214 F. 2d 962 (D.C. Circuit 1954).

blocks. First, the term "product" was excessively vague. Fanciful manipulation of psychodynamic personality theory could, and often did, result in a belief that virtually anything could cause anything. The second and perhaps more troubling aspect of the Durham rule was that at no point was the term "mental disease or defect" actually defined, which left each mental health professional with the task of defining it in every case. This clearly led to the unfortunate state of affairs, noted earlier, that there was no uniformity in the way examinations were conducted, no uniformity regarding the definition of mental disease or defect, and no uniformity in terms of the definition of "product."

The next major landmark decision in the field of criminal responsibility was the case of *McDonald vs. United States* (1962)[4] in which the court attempted to give a legal definition to the terms "mental disease or defect." It was defined as "any abnormal condition of the mind which substantially affects mental or emotional processes and substantially impairs behavioral controls." The intent of this definition was to narrow the scope of what mental disorders could be utilized in court in raising an insanity defense. In essence, it stated that not every diagnosable condition could result in a person's being exculpated of the crime but, rather, it would have to be a mental condition that revealed evidence of substantial impairment of mental or emotional processes and of behavioral controls. This still left unanswered the definition of "product." In courts that utilize the product test, one could hear judges rendering opinions about "product" using definitions that range from very narrow to exceedingly broad. Those judges instructing juries in a very broad sense would state that the jury should consider virtually anything in the defendant's history that relates to the criminal behavior, while those instructing jurors in the narrow sense construed product as a "but for" test (i.e., had the mental illness not existed, the person would not have committed this offense). One of the unfortunate consequences of the Durham rule and the inability to define the term "product" was that many courts determined that mental health professionals were taking a role away from the trier of fact, that the experts were rendering conclusory labels and that triers of fact, namely judges and juries, were merely rubber-stamping these opinions, not exercising their own judgment.

---

[4] *McDonald vs. U.S.,* 312 F. 2d 844 (D.C. Circuit 1962).

In *Washington vs. United States* (1967),[5] the court stated that an expert witness may testify about the development and adaptation of the individual, how the individual functioned and whether the particular disease or defect might conceivably impair her or his behavioral controls, but the expert was not to render the final "ultimate issue opinion" of whether or not the offense was a product of the mental disease or defect. This was regarded as a question for the triers of fact, who were supposed to evaluate and weigh all of the testimony, including the expert testimony.

Following Durham, as modified by both McDonald and Washington, the American Law Institute Model Penal Code (Section 4.01 - 1962) was adopted into Federal law in *U.S. vs. Brawner* (1972).[6] This standard spoke of an individual being not criminally responsible if, by reason of mental disease or defect, that individual lacked substantial capacity to appreciate the wrongfulness (sometimes called criminality) of her or his conduct, or lacked substantial capacity to conform her or his behavior to the requirements of the law. In some jurisdictions, there were statements added to this Code that allowed for the introduction of a concept of diminished capacity, namely that "as a result of a mental disease or defect, a person lacked the requisite specific intent to commit the alleged offense." This specific intent applies only to certain crimes and in such cases the mental disease or defect is regarded as a mitigating factor. Often, such a reduction of intent would be utilized in terms of sentencing or disposition rather than in a trial process itself. The ALI Model Penal Code also added the statement that diseases whose only manifestation was repeated criminal activity were specifically excluded from the purview of this test. In other words, this test eliminated the utilization of insanity defenses for people diagnosed as having antisocial, psychopathic or sociopathic personalities.

The ALI Model Penal Code remained in place in the Federal court system and was adopted by many state courts. It was not until 1981, following John Hinckley's attempt to assassinate President Ronald Reagan, that this standard came under scrutiny. Hinckley raised a defense of not guilty by reason of insanity and, indeed, was acquitted by reason of insanity in July of 1982. Hinckley had been tried in Federal court where the prosecution has to bear the burden of rebutting the insanity defense by the level of proof called "be-

---

[5] *Washington vs. U.S.*, 129 U.S. App. D.C. 29 (1967).
[6] *U.S. vs. Brawner*, 471 F. 2d 969 (D.C. Circ. 1972).

yond a reasonable doubt." Typically, in most state courts, the defense bears the burden by the lowest level of proof, "preponderance of evidence." There is also an intermediate level of proof described as "clear and convincing evidence." Many observers of the Hinckley trial believe that Hinckley's being found not guilty by reason of insanity was due to the Federal law itself: that it is virtually impossible for the prosecution to prove beyond a reasonable doubt that someone is insane when there is conflicting expert testimony. The public outcry over Hinckley's acquittal by reason of insanity led the Congress of the United States to start gathering information and debating the issue of changes in the Federal standard. The Congress solicited position papers from various professional organizations and what emerged was the Insanity Defense Reform Act of 1984. Although this Act is binding only on Federal courts, several states, notably California, have revised their insanity standards to come in line with the new Federal standard. This standard tracks the proposals submitted by both the American Psychiatric Association and the American Bar Association. The new standard would require evidence of a severe mental disease or defect that rendered an individual unable to appreciate the nature and quality or the wrongfulness of her or his act. This is basically a return to the original McNaughten standard and, in some ways, even more strict in that it specifies that the mental disease or defect must be severe. Both the American Bar Association and the American Psychiatric Association had recommended that the volitional prong of the ALI test, that part dealing with "lacking substantial capacity to conform one's behavior to the requirements of the law," be dropped. This was adopted and the test was restricted purely to cognition. It also shifted the burden of proof from the government to the defense, bringing it in line with the laws in most states. However, where the level of proof in most states was preponderance of evidence, the higher standard of clear and convincing evidence was used in the Insanity Defense Reform Act. The new standard does not allow the expert to render any testimony on ultimate issues, such as insanity or diminished capacity.

From the point of view of clinical implications of this Act, clinicians clearly will need to avoid any hint of addressing ultimate legal issues and will also need to be far more careful in looking at the criteria for insanity acquittal. Lack of impulse control, regardless of the basis for it, can no longer be considered in an insanity finding and the range of mental diseases or defects used to provide the basis for an insanity acquittal is also far more circumscribed. It is conceivable that avoiding ultimate issues may serve to force clinicians into utilizing uniform sources of data, and agreement may well rise among mental health experts on such cases, avoiding the problems posed by the so-called battle of the experts.

On the other hand, many clinicians who work in facilities governed by Federal law express grave reservations about the restrictions imposed by the Insanity Defense Reform Act. That is, one may, and often does, encounter an individual whose criminal behavior is clearly motivated by a delusional system but her or his behavior at the time of the offense clearly indicates the recognition of the wrongfulness of the behavior, despite its delusional underpinnings. The delusional thinking and its impelling or propelling the individual into the criminal activity would more than adequately be taken care of were there still a volitional prong to the test, but this has been abolished and eliminated. Clinicians working within these Federal settings are then faced with the uncomfortable dilemma of indicating that a chronically psychotic individual, whose behavior is motivated by a delusional system, may well be held responsible and accountable for her or his actions because their behavior at the time of the offense indicated some recognition of the wrongfulness of the behavior and even may have suggested some attempts to avoid detection. The following example will illustrate some of these dilemmas imposed by the Insanity Defense Reform Act of 1984.

The defendant, Mr. J, was a 30-year-old man, who developed a delusional system surrounding one of his neighbors, a federal judge. Mr. J became convinced that the judge was gay, interpreted several of the judge's friendly comments to him as evidence of his homosexual intentions and then regarded subsequent events as a result of his rejection of the judge's so-called advances. The defendant became more and more psychotic, with his behavior on the job becoming quite disorganized, and the result was his termination from that position. In his delusional thinking, he blamed the judge for his job termination, and believed that his neighbor was planning to kill him. He decided that he must retaliate against the judge in self-defense, because, within his delusional framework, he was fearful for his life.

The defendant obtained several cans of gasoline, waited until late at night, took a circuitous route from his home to his neighbor's home, set the judge's home on fire and then took an even more circuitous route from the judge's home back to his own home in order to avoid detection.

Had this been a case that could have been adjudicated under the old American Law Institute standard, the defendant's actions would clearly be seen as a product of his delusional system and one could argue that he, therefore, lacked substantial capacity to conform his behavior to the requirements of the law. However, since the victim in this case was a federal judge, the case was tried in federal court and the only issue of relevance was whether or not the defendant was aware of the wrongfulness of his actions. Waiting until it was dark outside and taking a circuitous route to and from the judge's house in order to avoid being detected indicated his awareness of the wrongfulness of his actions. Although under the old test he would be regarded as clearly not criminally responsible, the new Federal standard dictated that, he would have to be regarded as criminally responsible, an opinion which makes many clinicians, concerned with this individual's fragile mental state, quite distressed.

Chapter 4

ASSESSMENT
OF MALINGERING

Malingering represents a deliberate attempt to deceive, to create an impression of a mental disorder where none exists, or, more specifically regarding the issues which we are discussing here, to create the impression of a lack of criminal responsibility. There has been, within recent years, a great deal of well-validated empirical research on malingering and deception, as well as a refinement of the clinical methods of detecting its presence.[1, 2]

Assessment of malingering is perhaps one of the most difficult issues in the evaluation of criminal responsibility for an individual who has been trained in traditional clinical approaches. It requires a totally different "set" or "cognitive map" from that in psychotherapy or in psychological testing. In the traditional clinical setting, what the defendant reports is generally taken in a fairly straightforward manner, with the assessment of genuine and deliberate deception rarely being a significant part of the traditional clinical psychological undertaking. However, such an assessment is critical when doing a forensic examination. Especially in the area of assessment of criminal responsibility, if individuals can successfully feign a lack of criminal responsibility and are found not guilty by reason of insanity, they may petition the committing court for a release from the psychiatric facility because they do not meet the criteria for con-

---

[1] Malingering & Deception - An Update. (1990). *Behavioral Sciences and the Law,* 8(1).
[2] Rogers, R. (Ed.). (1997). *Clinical Assessment of Malingering and Deception* (2nd ed.). New York: Guilford.

tinued hospitalization. A recent Supreme Court decision (*Foucha vs. Louisiana,* 1992[3]) ruled that defendants can only be confined in a psychiatric facility if their "dangerousness" is due to a mental disease or defect rather than a personality disorder. Therefore, if a person with a personality disorder were to feign a mental illness in order to obtain an acquittal by reason of insanity, that person could no longer be confined within the psychiatric facility.

One caution needs to be observed, however. If a defendant is found to be malingering, it does not necessarily mean that there is *no* mental disorder. There may be an underlying mental disorder which is being exaggerated or the defendant may be malingering in order to avoid some deep-seated fears aroused by the incarceration, such as being homophobic.

In the assessment of malingering, there are many avenues of approach. The first is concerned with the necessity of doing a comprehensive examination over a period of time, preferably in a controlled institutional setting. As a practical matter, such examinations often cannot be made. There may be a limited period of time during which the defendant can be seen on only one or two occasions or for relatively brief interviews. On such occasions, it is crucial to obtain collateral material in order to gain a picture of whether the defendant in question acted in a similar manner prior to and following the evaluation. The best way of detecting malingering is through prolonged inpatient observation. Many defendants who come into a doctor's office for a pretrial criminal responsibility evaluation may try to appear far more disturbed than they are in reality. However, if the practitioner working in a hospital setting carefully documents not only the impressions given by the defendant in clinical interview but also compares and contrasts them with the defendant's behavior noted on the ward, interactions with family and friends during visiting hours and the behavior documented in nursing notes, the issue can often be clarified. For instance, if a defendant interacts in a coherent manner with staff, actively participates in ward activities and is able to discuss criminal charges with staff members but never with doctors, one needs to raise the question of malingering. When the discrepancies occur, and one can predict that the defendant will try to appear disturbed in court, all of the behaviors that one might expect should be documented in the court report and it should be pointed out that the behavior indicates deliberate attempts

---

[3] *Foucha vs. Louisiana,* 112 S.Ct. 1780 (1992).

at deception rather than being the outgrowth of a mental disease or defect. If the clinician has conducted an outpatient examination and has questions about malingering, no final opinion should be rendered at that point but rather the clinician should send a preliminary letter to the court indicating that the issue needs to be considered and that a period of inpatient hospitalization would be helpful in determining this.

If the defendant is incarcerated in a correctional setting, the practitioner needs to obtain whatever medical records are available and to interview various correctional personnel who have had contact with the individual. Certainly, family members and employers also need to be contacted to obtain their observations regarding the defendant's behavior in settings other than the one in which the examination is being conducted.

Sometimes, reviewing nursing notes will reveal discrepancies between the day-to-day behavior observed by the nursing staff and the doctor's opinion. A clinician would be well-advised, in reviewing the psychiatric record, to compare the actual dates of observations by the nursing staff with the same dates contained in the psychiatric or psychological evaluation for consistency or lack thereof between the two data sources. Another issue that can alert the clinician to the possibility of malingering is the nature of the symptom picture presented by the defendant. It is a relatively rare occurrence, for instance, for an individual attempting to feign mental disorders to know some of the subtleties that mental health professionals use to diagnose various clinical syndromes. For example, schizophrenia is generally characterized by auditory hallucinations and very rarely by visual hallucinations. Most defendants who are attempting to malinger by trying to appear schizophrenic are usually unaware of this distinction. Visual hallucinations are more characteristic of organically related psychoses and drug-induced psychoses. In addition, if a defendant claims to be experiencing auditory hallucinations, one needs to inquire what the voices are telling the defendant. Generally, since hallucinations represent the return of a repressed state that the person is unable to "keep buried" any longer, they will contain negative or derogatory self-references. If the defendant states that the voices tell her or him to do any variety of self-serving activities, such as "rob the bank," "bury the money" or "lock the door," the clinician needs to question seriously the validity of these reported hallucinatory experiences.

Other potentially valuable material in the assessment of malingering and psychosis may be derived from Exner's Comprehensive

System of Rorschach Scoring (Exner, 1985[4]) and the revised and expanded editions of that work (Exner, 1993[5]). It is far more difficult, if not impossible, for a defendant attempting to feign a mental disorder to imitate the formal structure rather than the content of psychotic thought. In other words, while an individual may give much bizarre and dramatic content on the Rorschach test, the formal structure of thought would not reveal impairment. Exner's scoring system for the Rorschach is particularly helpful in such cases because it has specific indices which point to various disturbances of thought that one would have in a genuine psychosis. Such features as deviant responding, deviant verbalizations, incongruent combinations, fabulized combinations, autistic logic and contamination are difficult features for someone who is not genuinely psychotic to imitate. As an example, if one were to try to imitate a looseness of association that might be tapped by the autistic logic score, it would come across in a somewhat stilted and anything but loose fashion. If there is an extreme discrepancy between many seemingly bizarre contents and few, if any, special scores whatsoever, the possibility of malingering needs to be suspected and further investigated.

A variety of early studies, based on content alone, suggested that Rorschach results could indeed be faked but, with the advent of Exner's comprehensive system utilizing formal structural scoring methods rather than an impressionistic, intuitive, content-based interpretation, it becomes easier to identify malingered profiles. Exner has noted, in fact, that malingerers may be identified by their use of good form responses but very dramatic verbiage. The first empirical study of Exner's concept for discrepancy between structural and content variables in malingered profiles was performed by Pettigrew et al. (1983).[6] The results of this study revealed that malingerers did indeed give significantly more good form with bizarre wording responses than did normal individuals or psychotics. Exner has asserted, in fact, that malingering of the Rorschach would be impossible if protocols were collected and scored according to the comprehensive system. Indeed, none of the reported studies which suggested

---

[4] Exner, J. (1985). *The Rorschach, A Comprehensive System* (Vol. I, 1st ed.). New York: Wiley.

[5] Exner, J. (1993). *The Rorschach, A Comprehensive System* (Vol. I, 2nd ed.). New York: Wiley.

[6] Pettigrew, C., Tuma, J., Pickering, J., & Whelton, J. (1983). Simultation of Psychosis on a Multiple Choice Prospective Test. *Perceptual and Motor Skills, 57,* 463-469.

that Rorschach responses could be faked utilized Exner's comprehensive system. There is clearly a need to replicate some of these early studies using Exner's comprehensive system but, from a clinical point of view, the distinction between bizarre content and an absence of special scores indicating psychotic thinking appears justified in determination of malingering. As this manuscript was being prepared, research on malingering utilizing the comprehensive system of Exner was being undertaken by Erdberg et al.

Resnick (1985)[7] suggested that a complete history of prior hallucinations and the defendant's reaction to the hallucinations should be obtained before asking the defendant anything regarding her or his mental state at the time of the alleged offense. A common error on the part of mental health professionals is the belief that psychotic patients must respond to the commands of the auditory hallucinations. In reality, research surveyed by Resnick found that psychotic patients generally ignored hallucinatory commands and suggestions. Resnick further noted that command hallucinations are usually associated with delusions and are related to some psychic purpose or meaning. Therefore, if the clinician observes a discrepancy or inconsistency between the characteristics or personality structure obtained through the psychological assessment and the apparent behavior at the time of the offense, malingering must also be suspected. As an example, if a psychological evaluation of a defendant reveals evidence of psychosis and bizarre thinking regarding issues of sexual identity, then these would need to be apparent in the person's motivation for the crime. If this same individual, on the other hand, is charged with robbing a bank and asserts that "the voices" told him to "rob the bank and bury the money," one would suspect malingering because of the discrepancy between the personality structure and the alleged hallucination.

The clinician can construct a checklist regarding hallucinations, asking the individual whether or not she or he must always respond to the commands of the auditory hallucinations, what the individual can do to make the hallucinations go away and whether the hallucinations are intermittent or continuous (the same research points to the fact that genuine hallucinations tend to diminish when patients are involved in activities). In other words, reports of auditory hallucinations which are questionable and raise the possibility of malingering are those that patients describe as continuous, vague or

[7] Resnick, P. (1985). Malingered Psychosis. *Behavioral Sciences and the Law,* 3(1), 21-38.

inaudible; not associated with delusions or described in stilted language in which instructions are always obeyed and for which there are no strategies to diminish the voices.

Finally, malingerers tend to overact and attempt to call attention to their illnesses in contrast to genuinely psychotic patients who prefer to deny or hide or, at the least, be reluctant to discuss their symptoms. A malingerer's symptoms often fit into no known diagnostic entity and delusional systems generally develop quite gradually over time, while malingerers frequently will claim the sudden development of a delusional system. Again, one caution is in order, in that the "sudden onset" variety of delusional thinking is at times associated with drug-induced psychoses and therefore should not automatically be dismissed as malingering.

On occasion, in assessing criminal responsibility, the clinician will encounter an individual who is claiming to be a multiple personality, stating that there is an innocent or good personality and an offender or bad personality who committed the crime. Resnick (1985)[8] provides some very intriguing observations on the malingering of multiple personality disorder. Initially, he notes that malingerers experience difficulty being consistent in the voice of the assumed personality, as well as with movement characteristics and other aspects of memory. Malingerers rarely will present historical evidence of multiple personalities prior to the event in question, while genuine cases often will have other evidence of the alters, such as separate wardrobes and separate diaries. When asked to recount life events, malingerers often do not report life events common in genuine multiple personalities, such as finding objects in one's possession for which one cannot account or refractory somatic symptoms. In sharp distinction to the good and bad personality often attempted by the malingerer, a genuine multiple personality disorder patient will appear bewildered by the apparent criminal activity. In fact, personalities other than the offender personality may, in a self-destructive way, accept the blame and become depressed and suicidal. Once again, consistent with the tendency noted above of overacting, malingerers will attempt to exaggerate the symptoms, while true patients with multiple personalities tend to hide the symptoms. In genuine multiple personality disorder, the primary or host personality is often unaware of the existence of alters, while most frequently the malingerer seems to be quite aware of all of them.

---

[8] *Ibid*, pp. 21-38.

ASSESSMENT AND DETECTION
OF MALINGERED AMNESIA

In forensic settings, especially when conducting criminal responsibility evaluations, the clinician will often encounter the defendant who states that she or he does not remember anything about the offense. When defendants display memory deficits of a type or severity that make no sense in terms of the clinical history, the possibility of malingering or purposeful exaggeration of memory loss must be investigated. This certainly implies that a careful clinical history needs to be taken prior to an assessment of memory of the alleged offense. Wiggins and Brandt (1988)[9] demonstrated that specific questions in a clinical interview format help distinguish genuine from malingered amnesia. The questions were very simple for even moderately impaired individuals suffering from genuine amnesia. Questions involved such areas as name, age, birth date, telephone number, address, Social Security number, mother's first name, mother's maiden name, father's first name and names of brothers or sisters, as well as what food the individual ate for breakfast and for the previous night's dinner. Even those with significant brain damage could recall virtually all of the items of personal identity, while those simulating amnesia significantly missed a large number of the items.

Brandt also described more experimental approaches which are generally based on the hypothesis that the malingerer who is unfamiliar with the symptoms of genuine amnesia will tend to overplay the role and perform memory tasks more poorly than people suffering from genuine amnesia. This is consistent with Resnick's description of the malingerer as one who tends to overact or exaggerate the part. Some of the studies even note that the malingerers perform at a level below that expected by chance and that even patients with the most severe chronic global amnesia can learn new information and display the effects of learning experiences when tested appropriately, while malingerers fail to demonstrate this ability at all.

---

[9] Wiggins, E., & Brandt, J. (1988). Detection of Simulated Amnesia. *Law and Human Behavior, 12*(1), 57-78.

USE OF MMPI IN THE
ASSESSMENT OF MALINGERING

Green (1988)[10] observes that in the development of the Minnesota Multiphasic Personality Inventory (MMPI), Meehl and Hathaway pointed to the necessity of evaluating two defense styles which they described as faking bad and faking good. Initially, the L, F and K scales served as validity measures. The L scale, measuring social desirability, included a list of extremely desirable but very rare human qualities. A high score on the L scale indicated defensiveness. The F scale included items that were answered with a relatively low frequency by a majority of the normative group and the K scale was proposed as a suppressor variable. In addition, there has been some research examining endorsement on subtle versus obvious items on five of the MMPI clinical scales: depression, hysteria, psychopathic deviate, paranoia and hypomania. These scales and the use of these items tended to be helpful in identifying both malingering and defensiveness. Summing the differences between the obvious and subtle T score scales is one suggested method. An individual attempting to malinger, deceive or exaggerate will clearly have elevated obvious items and depressed subtle items, while an individual who is defensive will have exactly the opposite pattern. Green suggested that a sum of difference scores between subtle and obvious items in the range of 250 to 300 was strongly suggestive of malingering, though some question remained about what the lower limit for classifying a malingered profile would be. Green also discussed the Gough Dissimulation Scale[11] consisting of 74 items, later revised in the Dissimulation Scale Revised (DS-R) to 40 items, which significantly differentiated a group of genuine patients from groups of college students and professional psychologists instructed to simulate the responses of neurotic patients. Of some interest is that there does not appear to be a great overlap between the items on the Dissimulation Scale and those items suggesting extreme or severe psychopathology. The elevation on the DS-R scale, coupled with a relatively low F scale and an insignificant difference on the subtle and obvious items, for instance, may suggest an individual who is not trying

---

[10] Greene, R. L. (1988). Assessment of Malingering and Defensiveness by Objective Personality Measures. In R. Rogers (Ed.), *Clinical Assessment of Malingering and Deception* (pp. 123-158). New York: Guilford.

[11] Gough, H. G. (1947). Simulated Patterns on the MMPI. *Journal of Abnormal and Social Psychology, 42,* 215-225.

to feign extreme psychopathology but rather is seeking to bring attention to her or his distress and to assume a passive and helpless role. As such, the DS-R scale could be seen as relevant to factitious disorder and to issues of secondary gain, rather than to deliberate exaggeration of gross psychopathology. In addition, the MMPI-2[12] has a variety of other scales, such as variable response inconsistency (VRIN) and true response inconsistency (TRIN), which can be helpful in distinguishing whether the abnormally high number of unusual items endorsed is a function of deliberate exaggeration, attempting to attain the "patient role" or whether it is due to misunderstanding the items on the test. Clearly, if one uses the MMPI or MMPI-2, it should be one of many different assessment devices for malingering and the different combinations of validity scales need to be utilized. Therefore, even when we break it down into specific tests, these tests must be used in a comprehensive manner, not depending on any one score.

NEUROPSYCHOLOGICAL ASSESSMENT

The previously noted difficulty of not relying on any single test becomes especially crucial in neuropsychological assessment. Neuropsychological test batteries are important because generally the wider range of behaviors sampled and the greater the degree of inconsistency between tasks presumably measuring the same function, the greater the indications of malingering. Neuropsychological assessment is most helpful in the examination of a malingerer when the clinician understands the underlying neurological pathology. One needs to consider the history of the patient and the specific nature of the alleged dysfunction: Is the patient displaying deficits compatible with the disorder that she or he is attempting to feign? One needs to observe discrepancies between different tests and the nature of the responding. Patients complaining of memory loss frequently fail many items on general information and comprehension subtests not understanding the difference between short- and long-term memory. In addition, one must look at the inconsistencies between the patient's activities and test performances. For example, a patient seen by this author described total memory loss regarding

[12] Hathaway, S. R., McKinley, J. C., & Butcher, J. N. (1989). *Minnesota Multiphasic Personality Inventory - 2.* Minneapolis, MN: University of Minnesota Press.

the alleged offense but was able to make three bus transfers in order to get to the author's office, raising serious questions about malingering. Schretlen[13] describes the development of a test battery which included an MMPI, Bender-Gestalt and a malingering scale developed specifically for this study. The malingering scale consisted of four subtests, vocabulary, abstraction, arithmetic and information, and consisted of 90 items that required about 20 minutes to complete. Most of the items were adapted from existing intelligence scales, while others were rationally derived. The majority of items are easy enough to be passed by an average person and the items are not arranged in hierarchial order. The information and arithmetic subtests are administered verbally, much the same as the Wechsler subtests with the same names, and the vocabulary and abstraction subtests consist of two alternative forced choice items. All items are scored 0 or +1 with no time requirements or speed bonuses, and scores are obtained by summing the number of correct answers on each subtest. Schretlen found that the subjects who feigned insanity scored significantly higher than psychiatric inpatients. Genuine patients had a mean of 63 and a standard deviation of 20, while the feigners had a mean of 87 and a standard deviation of 4. Features of the Bender-Gestalt which tended to differentiate malingerers from nonmalingerers were inhibited figure size, distorted relationships, gross simplification and inconsistent form quality.

The Structured Interview of Reported Symptoms (SIRS)

The Structured Interview of Reported Symptoms (SIRS) by Rogers[14] is perhaps the most widely recognized and best validated instrument for the detection of malingering and deception. It is a structured interview format that contains a variety of items from different assessment instruments. It also includes measures of consistency and appears to have adequate predictive validity and a high inter-rater reliability. Rogers describes eight primary scales and five supplementary scales. The primary scales include a rare symptom scale which contains symptoms occurring very infrequently in

---

[13] Schretlen, D. (1990). A Psychological Test Battery to Detect Prison Inmates Who Fake Insanity or Mental Retardation. *Behavioral Sciences and the Law, 8*(1), 75-84.

[14] Rogers, R. (1992). *Structured Interview of Reported Symptoms (Manual)*. Odessa, FL: Psychological Assessment Resources.

bona fide patients. The symptom combination scale consists of item pairs of common psychiatric problems that rarely occurred simultaneously. A scale called Improbable and Absurd Symptoms consists of symptoms which have a fantastic or preposterous quality rendering them by definition unlikely to be true. The Blatant Symptoms scale consists of symptoms that untrained individuals would likely identify as obvious signs of mental illness. The Subtle Symptoms scale consists of symptoms that untrained individuals are more likely to associate with every day problems of minor maladjustments than with a major mental illness. Selectivity of Symptoms is comprised of the combination of Blatant and Subtle Symptom scales and indicates an indiscriminate endorsement of psychological or psychiatric problems. The Severity of Symptoms scale consists of the number of blatant and subtle symptoms that are endorsed at a level of extreme or unbearable severity. The Reported versus Observed Symptoms scale is based on a comparison of the patient's observable behavior and her or his responses to the items. Supplemental scales include Direct Appraisal of Honesty, items addressing the patient's willingness to be self-disclosing, Defensive Symptoms which represents many every day problems and worries that most individuals have experienced and the Overly Specified Symptoms scale which consists of symptoms described with an unrealistic degree of precision, typically indicating an implausible attempt to quantify an emotional problem. Finally, there is a Symptom Onset and Resolution scale that consists of items reflecting sudden atypical changes in the course of a mental disorder and an Inconsistency of Symptoms scale which contains items identical to those in the Blatant and Subtle scales, repeated as a measure of discordant self-reporting. The scores are then plotted and each of the primary scales reveals a score in a range called *honest responding, indeterminate responding, probable malingering* and *definite malingering*. Rogers presents a great deal of research regarding the likelihood of feigning based on a combination of certain scaled scores in the probable feigning range, as well as the likelihood of honest responding based on a combination of SIRS scaled scores in the honest responding range. Rogers notes, however, that there are occasionally cases in which a client's responses strongly suggest feigning, yet she or he does not meet the criterion of definite feigning on either a single scale or combination of scales. In these cases, Rogers suggests the computation of a total score and notes that the upper range on total SIRS scores for honest responders are less than or equal to 71. With a five-point buffer, a criterion of greater than 76 will classify feigning based on total SIRS

scores. Using this criterion, Rogers found that 38.9% suspected malingerers and 56.6% simulators were correctly identified as feigning. It has been this author's experience that the use of this total
SIRS score in what Rogers calls "nebulous cases" is, in fact, the
approach most frequently needed.

Chapter 5

FORMAL ASSESSMENT OF CRIMINAL RESPONSIBILITY: THE ROGERS CRIMINAL RESPONSIBILITY ASSESSMENT SCALE

This chapter will discuss the structure of an instrument designed by Richard Rogers to "provide a systematic and reliable model for evaluating patients for criminal responsibility."[1] The following two chapters will describe a less structured interview format developed by this author, which covers many of the same dimensions from a slightly different vantage point.

The Rogers Criminal Responsibility Assessment Scale (R-CRAS) contains scales measuring patient reliability, organic impairment, presence of major mental illness, cognitive control and behavioral control at the time of the alleged offense. Descriptive criteria for each of the scales are provided. The first part of the test attempts to establish the degree of impairment on psychological variables which would figure in the determination of insanity. The second part describes the decision process used to render an accurate opinion on criminal responsibility using the previously discussed ALI standard. This part also includes decision models for rendering opinions in cases where the McNaughten standard is used and where a guilty but mentally ill verdict is being used.

Consistent with the model proposed earlier, Rogers notes a number of important dimensions at the beginning, including psychiatric evaluations, psychological evaluations, relevant social histories,

---

[1] Rogers, R. (1984). *Rogers Criminal Responsibility Assessment Scale, Interpretive Manual.* Odessa, FL: Psychological Assessment Resources.

relevant police reports, collateral interviews, test scores, employment and occupational history, whether or not there has been a prior finding of incompetence to stand trial, the length of time between the evaluation and the commitment of the offense, history of alcohol or drug abuse or dependence and the number of arrests both as a juvenile and as an adult. A listing of the offense and behavior prior to, during and after the offense are also utilized as "situational information."

With this background material prepared, the examiner is asked to rate the reliability of the patient's self-report under voluntary control all the way from a reliable self-report to definite malingering, and then to also rate the degree of interference with reliability on an involuntary basis, that is, some mental state that interferes with an accurate memory of the alleged crime. Once again, this is rated from none to severe involuntary interference, and is also assessed in a similar manner, namely, degree of impairment: level of intoxication, evidence of brain impairment, relationship of brain impairment to the offense, level of mental retardation, relationship of mental retardation to the commission of the offense, observable bizarre behavior at the time of the offense, level of anxiety at the time of the offense, amnesia for the offense, delusions, hallucinations, depressed mood, elevated or expansive mood, level of verbal coherence, intensity of affect and evidence of formal thought disorder at the time of the alleged offense. The examiner is then asked to rate dimensions such as planning and preparation for the offense, awareness of criminality during the commission of the offense, the degree of intentionality at the time of the offense, the level of activity, the degree of impairment in non-offense-related activities prior to the offense, reported and observed self-control over the criminal behavior and whether or not loss of control, if any, was the result of a psychosis.

Rogers then provides additional assessment criteria for the guilty but mentally ill and McNaughten decision models, noting that at the time of the preparation of the manual that its use should be restricted to research. Here again, Rogers provides detailed descriptions of impaired judgment, psychopathologically impaired behavior, impairment of reality testing and capacity for self-care at the time of the alleged crime. An additional assessment criterion for the McNaughten standard deals with awareness of the wrongfulness of the alleged criminal behavior.

Finally, the decision models represent a summation of the scores on the various dimensions.

Chapter 6
CONSISTENCY
ACROSS DATA SOURCES

Previously described has been a model suggested by this author in which multiple data sources are utilized in what could best be described as a hypothesis-generating model. That is, a given source of data (e.g., clinical interview, history taking, psychological testing, review of prior psychiatric/psychological records) gives rise to a hypothesis or series of hypotheses which will be subject to verification or lack of verification by observing whether or not the hypotheses stand up over the course of several different areas of inquiry. Only those that do stand up in this manner will go into the final assessment and formulation. Those that do not will be discarded. The final opinion on criminal responsibility, therefore, will reflect a consistency across multiple data sources. If the data is inconsistent, however, this will be noted in the conclusion, and the conclusion will be appropriately qualified in terms of the data that is missing or the data which is inconsistent. Not only will this yield opinions with far more credibility and integrity for the individual doing the forensic assessment, it is a requirement of the current Ethical Principles of Psychologists and Code of Conduct (1992). Recall that that document, as well as others, such as the Specialty Guidelines for Forensic Psychologists, discuss the need to appropriately limit conclusions in terms of the reliability and validity of the data, to render conclusions only when there is sufficient data to back up those conclusions or recommendations and to actively test competing hypotheses and seemingly contradictory sources of data.

While this model has been discussed earlier as a very valuable one in the assessment of malingering, it can also be seen as very helpful, in fact essential, toward the preparation of an overall opinion regarding criminal responsibility.

Consider, for example, the case in which an individual charged with an offense has had an extensive history of psychiatric hospitalization. The hypothesis, of course, to be looked at is whether or not the mental disorder with which the individual had been diagnosed bears any causal relationship to the offense. In order to do this, the examiner must first look at the kinds of behaviors documented in the psychiatric record to determine what the typical behavior of that individual was while the person was demonstrating signs of the mental disorder. In other words, do the hospital records and history reveal that, at the time of the acute presence of symptoms, the individual was agitated, withdrawn, assaultive, fearful, delusional, hallucinating and so on. Once a coherent picture of this individual's behavior while overtly mentally ill is gained, the examiner can then use these impressions as a basis for interviews with family, friends, witnesses, arresting police officers and so on, to ascertain whether the behaviors typical of the individual's mental disorder were present or absent at the time of the commission of the offense. This material is further refined by results of psychological testing, neuropsychological assessment, neurological evaluation and the results of various physical examinations. As noted above, the examiner is always looking for consistencies across all of the data sources. For example, if a defendant had an established history of severe mental disorder which was characterized by his huddling in a corner, being preoccupied and fearful, and the behavior demonstrated at the time of the offense was highly intentional, purposeful and goal-directed, the examiner would have to question whether or not there was a clear linkage or consistency between the mental disorder and the crime. In the case described, the examiner might well have to conclude, if the inconsistency existed, that while the defendant had a history of mental disorder, the behavior demonstrated at the time of the offense did not appear to be consistent with the manifestations of that disorder in this particular patient, and that therefore a causal link could not be established. This could well result in an opinion that in fact the individual was, despite the mental disorder, criminally responsible or that there was not enough data available to render an opinion on criminal responsibility. The forensic examiner must be willing to state in many cases that not enough data is available to render a conclusion.

In a similar manner, as noted in an earlier example, a defendant may have a long established history of mental illness characterized by doubts about his sexuality, these concerns being manifested not only in hospital records and in interviews with friends and family, but on the psychological testing. When the offense with which he is charged is, for instance, bank robbery and he tells the examiner that "the voices" told him to rob the bank, this clearly represents an inconsistency between the established history of mental illness and the behavior at the time of the offense. Once again, the discrepancy needs to be noted. Of course, were the examiner rendering an opinion in a state that has the guilty but mentally ill option, then the inconsistency between the behavior at the time of the offense and the mental illness could well not be that significant. The examiner would merely indicate the behavior at the time of the offense and the history of the underlying mental disorder and not need to make any causal link between the two.

Finally, let us assume that an individual has had a persistent history of delusions and hallucinations with religious overtones such that he feels he has a certain mission, characterized by his need to destroy certain established religions and provide sacrifices as evidence of his commitment to his new religious beliefs. This individual is charged with defacing a church and attempting to sacrifice his son by baking him in an oven. In this case, the causal link could be far more clearly drawn. If the same individual, however, attempts to rob an individual at gunpoint or at knifepoint, it is highly unlikely that the delusional religious beliefs had anything to do with the offense itself. One factor which must be kept in mind is that many elements come to play in a person's motivation for committing a criminal offense. The presence of an active mental illness does *not* necessarily mean that it is the mental illness which caused the criminal behavior.

This multiple data source approach also highlights another point made earlier, that one simply cannot overgeneralize from findings from any one data source but must constantly integrate those findings with a variety of other sources.

One of the most frequent areas in which this occurs is in the use and misuse of psychological testing. Individuals who do not have training in forensic settings will often conduct a battery of psychological testing, observe a particular degree of impairment on the testing and conclude, with no further data input, that that impairment must have been present at the time of the alleged offense. Such conclusions simply cannot be drawn.

It should also be noted, as mentioned in the introduction to this manual, that, especially in light of recent court decisions, forensic examiners need to move toward what could best be described as a "standard of care" in doing an assessment of criminal responsibility.

Several courts, in fact, have recognized what appropriate forensic evaluation entails and how traditional psychiatric and psychological evaluations often fall short of those evaluations in legal settings. While it is beyond the scope of this brief manual to discuss these cases in much detail, the reader is referred to *Strozier vs. Georgia* (1985) and *Illinois vs. Smith* (1984), discussed earlier, to note the court's dim view of experts who depend exclusively on their clinical assessments, not consulting any secondary sources of data.

As noted earlier, in addition to the ethical strictures which indicate to us that we may base our conclusions only on data sufficient to support the conclusions, there is the practical matter that the consistency across data sources protects the forensic expert from the typical onslaught of cross-examination in which opposing counsel inevitably confronts the expert with all of the things that she or he "didn't do but should have done."

Ziskin (1988)[1] provides a rather compelling series of questions that an aggressive attorney may use in attempting to undercut expert testimony. Though Ziskin's material renders many experts quite fearful of testifying, the consistency across data approach described previously in which psychological material must have real world correlates can go a long way toward defusing such an attack. Faust,[2] an associate of Ziskin, in fact conceded that integrating multiple sources of data and qualifying conclusions in light of inconsistent data would go a long way toward reducing the criticisms of expert testimony made by them. Their critique is, upon careful reading, based on the inappropriate overgeneralization from limited data without qualification, the very approach eschewed by this book.

---

[1] Ziskin, J., & Faust, D. (1988). *Coping With Psychiatric and Psychological Testimony* (5th ed.). Los Angeles: Law and Psychology Press.
[2] Faust, D. (1990). *The Validity of Forensic Assessment.* Discussion at the American Psychological Association Convention in Boston, MA.

Chapter 7

STRUCTURE OF
THE EXAMINATION

In this last chapter, I will attempt to integrate the material from the previous chapters into what I call a forensic evaluation outline. Here, in one document, will be contained the basis of the material for a comprehensive criminal responsibility assessment for each section of the outline. (See Forensic Evaluation Outline - Appendix D on pp. 79-103).

1. Basic demographic data, consisting of the defendant's name, date of birth, age, birth order, place of birth, religion, marital status, occupation, race and present living arrangement, need initially to be provided. A careful listing of the charges can also go in this section.

2. A section needs to be included which indicates the documents reviewed and people interviewed. This section will refer to all of the family, friends, employers, police officers and other people with whom interviews have been conducted, as well as all of the records reviewed, which will generally include police reports, witness statements, psychiatric history, medical history (if relevant) and other materials received from the referring party.

3. The section on confidentiality/privilege waiver is quite important. This may be done either with a formal waiver of privilege document (Appendix C on pp. 73-78), though very frequently defendants are loathe to sign such documents. If there is not such a document in the record, there should be a very careful statement, preferably in the defendant's own words, within the examiner's notes, of the defendant's un-

derstanding of the lack of confidentiality in the examination, and to whom the results of the examination will be disclosed and under what circumstances. In light of previous discussion about court decisions limiting testimony of experts when such informed consent has not been obtained, this is a very important section of the assessment to have well-documented.

4. Statement of facts. This section consists largely of a summary of police reports, witness' statements, interviews of police officers and witnesses and results of drug and alcohol screening tests if the results of those are available. Not only does this put in context several observations of behavior but does provide some documentation whether bizarre behavior, if observed, might be attributed to drug or alcohol intoxication.

5. Defendant's version of offense. This section includes material, suggested by Rogers in his instrument, concerning the nature of behavior in the week preceding the offense.

6. Behavior in jail. This is a very important section because it will highlight the possibility of a patient's deterioration or decompensation in jail as compared or contrasted with someone who was apparently psychotic at the time of the commission of an offense. Include in this section the defendant's statements, as well as interviews of correctional officers.

7. Jail psychiatric records. Check to see whether the defendant has requested psychiatric consultation or whether any of her or his behavior has come to the attention of the medical or psychiatric personnel in the jail. Include here a discussion of psychiatric consultations, medication, diagnosis and, perhaps most importantly, consistency or inconsistency with the behavior documented in the previous section.

8. Mental status examination. This, of course, refers to the mental status of the individual at the time of the examination of her or him and will include such dimensions as appearance, behavior, orientation, attention, perception, memory, affect, speech, presence of delusions, hallucinations or suicidal ideation, judgment, indications of toxicity, insight and estimated level of intellectual functioning.

9. Social history. The social history can be obtained from the defendant and consistencies or inconsistencies derived from interviews with family and friends should be included in this section. A subsection of this will deal with early childhood and include family composition, nature of interactions, in-

tactness of the family, major events, illnesses and injuries. A section on latency age should include school performance. With reference to school records, attempts should be made to obtain them. If they were made available, include the defendant's attitude toward her or his studies, outside interests and the nature of peer interactions. Similarly, a discussion of the adolescent years should include sexual development, identity issues, drug and alcohol use or abuse, nature of peer interactions and any jobs held. A section on young adulthood should describe the nature of interpersonal relationships and quality of job history, and, of course, this should be brought up to date with a section on adulthood.

10. Some examiners may prefer to break the social history down into various content areas rather than ages and a possible alternative would be to deal with sexual and marital history, education, vocation, military history, religious history and drug and alcohol abuse. Following this format, the examiner should include under sexual and marital, dating patterns, number of marriages, personality of spouses and reasons for separation, if any. Under education would be included types of schools (especially if special education is involved), grades and extracurricular activities. The vocational section would include number of jobs and length of jobs to give some indication of whether or not there has been job stability. The military history would include branch of service, dates served, rank attained and a potentially very important source of data would be disciplinary actions, if any. Religious history is, of course, self-explanatory and under drug and alcohol history, one would want to include the history, the age at which the abuse began, the extent of the drug or alcohol abuse and its typical effects on behavior.

11. Criminal history. Under this section attempt to ascertain both from the defendant and from criminal history reports the date of the offense, the place of the offense (that is, the state or county or city), the charges and the disposition.

12. Psychiatric history. This section should actually have two parts, dealing with the person's own psychiatric history and, if relevant, psychiatric history of any other family members. Here the nature of the admission should be inquired into, that is, whether it was voluntary or involuntary, and whether or not the defendant is willing to sign releases for the examiner to obtain these records. The type of treatment is also

important to determine, whether or not the defendant was treated primarily with medication, with psychotherapy or with some combination of the two. The family psychiatric history, of course, may not be quite as reliable, largely because the records may be unavailable and releases may not be able to be obtained, and therefore this section may need to be obtained by a description from the defendant and, if possible, through family interviews. A recommended format for the disclosure of records is included here. This format is broad enough to include the obtaining of various other kinds of records that have already been described.

13. Neurological history. This section is not intended to be a comprehensive neurological examination due to the fact that most people conducting such examinations are not trained neurologists. Nevertheless, there should be a review of certain symptoms and of certain historical data which would alert the forensic evaluator to the need for more complete neurological evaluation or neuropsychological assessment. Clearly, a history of head injuries and sequelae of the head injuries need to be determined as precisely as possible. These would include the details of the injuries and the hospitals where treatment was rendered, with an attempt to obtain these records later. Typical symptoms following head injuries, such as blackouts, dizzy spells, seizures, staring spells, repetitive stereotyped movements and perceptual distortions should be inquired into carefully. In addition, phenomena such as pathological intoxication, spatial disorientation, explosive behavioral outbursts, confusional episodes, fugue states, *déjà vu* and *jamais vu* experiences should be carefully explored. Learning disabilities need to be inquired into, though these may well be unrelated to any history of trauma. Other symptoms to be inquired about would be symptoms of depersonalization, blurriness of vision, history of delirium tremens, disturbances of memory, difficulties in attending to oral or written communication, a history of venereal disease and contact with certain toxic chemicals.

14. Sections are then provided for a concise summary of psychiatric records, medical records, interviews with treating therapists, occupational records, school records and other evaluations in the current case. As noted earlier, in discussion of the Specialty Guidelines for Forensic Psychologists, this should not be an opportunity for a "free-for-all" attack on the

opposing expert but rather for a comparison and contrast of the data obtained by another examiner and by the present forensic examiner. For instance, if a previous examiner has MMPI or Rorschach data which presents a clearly pathological profile and this material is absent in the current evaluation, this would be important data worth noting here. Similarly, if the previous data appears to be relatively intact and the data which the current examiner has obtained shows some degree of deterioration, this should also be noted in this section.

15. If the individual defendant has been referred for certain consultations, for instance, a neurological evaluation, a section is provided for a summary of these examinations.

16. A section which describes in detail the results of a psychological test battery should be included here. As a prelude to this section, the examiner should discuss the defendant's test-taking attitude, behavior demonstrated, degree of defensiveness, motivation, as well as such issues as validity, reaction time and perseveration. There should be a discussion of the various test instruments used, including the intelligence testing, projective and objective personality testing, neuropsychological screening, a comprehensive neuropsychological battery if utilized and an assessment of malingering, whether based on a formal instrument such as the Structured Interview of Reported Symptoms or on the examiner's observations.

In making the final recommendation regarding criminal responsibility, the issue that should always be kept in mind is how the mental disorder relates to each of the functional capacities, namely, how a person's delusions, hallucinations, loose associations or other impairment of thought processes would affect her or his ability to appreciate the wrongfulness of the behavior or the ability to conform the behavior to the requirements of the law, if applicable (i.e., if this is not in a Federal court). This largely goes back to the issue of whether or not one should render an opinion on the so-called "ultimate issue." It is my contention, as I have described before, that these are, in fact, not ultimate issues and that as long as one provides the data upon which the conclusions are based, it is permissible to answer questions about appreciation of wrongfulness and ability to conform to the law. (Appendix E on pp. 105-156 contains four sample reports.)

TABLE OF CONTENTS
FOR APPENDICES

61

APPENDIX A

Sample Letter to Attorney Regarding
<u>Release of Raw Data</u>

DAVID L. SHAPIRO, PHD
DIPLOMATE IN FORENSIC PSYCHOLOGY
AMERICAN BOARD OF PROFESSIONAL PSYCHOLOGY
1498-M REISTERTOWN ROAD
MAIL BOX 274
BALTIMORE, MARYLAND 21208

Telephone: (410) 653-5673

January 11, 1999

Harry Smith, Esquire
100 South Main Street
Chicago, IL 00000

Dear Mr. Smith:

I am in receipt of your subpoena dated _____ demanding production of "all records, notes, reports and files regarding the (treatment), (examination) and/or (evaluation) of _____."

Pursuant to the Ethical Principles of Psychologists and Code of Conduct and the General Guidelines for Providers of Psychological Services, I am enclosing all materials with the exception of the raw psychological test data.

Ethical Standards 2.02(b) and 2.06 require me to release such data only to another psychologist qualified to interpret such data. General Guideline 2.3.7 essentially states the same principle.

If you would please provide me the name and address of the psychologist whom you have retained to review this data, I will promptly forward copies of all such data to her or him.

I trust that you understand the ethical constraints described above.

Thank you in advance for your cooperation.

Very truly yours,

David L. Shapiro, PhD
Diplomate in Forensic Psychology
American Board of Professional
Psychology

DLS:esp

Enclosures

65

APPENDIX B

Motion for Protective Order

	*	IN THE
State of _____	*	CIRCUIT COURT
vs.	*	FOR (County)
Defendant	*	Case No. _____

*   *   *   *   *   *   *   *   *

MOTION FOR PROTECTIVE ORDER AND RESPONSE OF DAVID L. SHAPIRO, PhD TO MOTION TO COMPEL PRODUCTION OF DOCUMENTS

Now comes David L. Shapiro, PhD, by his attorney, _____, and pursuant to (State), (Federal) Rule _____, hereby moves for a Protective Order against providing "raw" psychological data to a nonpsychologist, and for the reasons, states:

1.   The subpoena sought by the (Defendant), (Government) was to produce copies of "all records, notes, reports and files regarding the treatment, examination and/or evaluation of _____ _____."

2.   David L. Shapiro, PhD, a clinical psychologist, in response to the subpoena provided all records, notes and reports with the exception of the "raw data" of the psychological tests administered to _____.

3.   Doctor Shapiro explained to (Defendant's Counsel), (Government) that the <u>Ethical Principles of Psychologists and Code</u>

of Conduct and General Guidelines of his profession require that such "raw data" only be released to another licensed psychologist who has training in psychological testing. Copies of Principle 2.3.7 of the General Guidelines and 2.02(b) and 2.06 of the Ethical Principles are attached herein as Exhibit A.

4.   Doctor Shapiro attempted to both comply with the subpoena and the ethical requirements by explaining the conflict to Ms./Mr. _____ and suggesting an alternate means to secure the records (_____ letter of _____ to Ms./Mr. _____ attached as Exhibit B).

5.   No response was had to Doctor Shapiro's letter of _____ with the exception of the filing of a Motion to Compel Production of Documents.

6.   Were Ms./Mr. _____ to designate a psychologist for the forwarding of the raw data, Doctor Shapiro will gladly forward such data as per the letter of _____.

WHEREFORE, David L. Shapiro, PhD, requests the following:

A.   Granting of a Protective Order providing that the "raw data" only be released to a psychologist;

B.   Denial of the Motion to Compel Production of Documents; and,

C.   Grant such other and further relief as the nature of this cause may require.

Respectfully submitted,

_____

Attorney for

David L. Shapiro, PhD

APPENDIX C

Informed Consent to Forensic
<u>Evaluation: Sample Documents</u>

DAVID L. SHAPIRO, PhD
DIPLOMATE IN FORENSIC PSYCHOLOGY
AMERICAN BOARD OF PROFESSIONAL PSYCHOLOGY
1498-M REISTERTOWN ROAD
MAIL BOX 274
BALTIMORE, MARYLAND 21208

Telephone: (410) 653-5673

INFORMED CONSENT TO FORENSIC EVALUATION:
ATTORNEY-CLIENT PRIVILEGE

I, _____, have been informed by Doctor David Shapiro of the nature of this examination, namely an assessment of my mental status regarding the issue of (competency to stand trial), (criminal responsibility), (sentencing). I understand that this is not a doctor-patient relationship bound by the traditional rules of confidentiality. I understand that Doctor Shapiro will be writing a report based on my assessment and will be sending a copy of that report to my attorney. I further understand that if my attorney and I desire to utilize Doctor Shapiro's report or testimony in court, then a copy of his report will be revealed to the government's attorney. Otherwise, the report and conclusions will remain with my attorney alone. I understand that the decision to utilize this material in court is a decision to be made by my attorney and by me.

_____   _____
Date   Signature

                                               _____
                                               Witness

75

DAVID L. SHAPIRO, PHD
DIPLOMATE IN FORENSIC PSYCHOLOGY
AMERICAN BOARD OF PROFESSIONAL PSYCHOLOGY
1498-M REISTERTOWN ROAD
MAIL BOX 274
BALTIMORE, MARYLAND 21208

Telephone: (410) 653-5673

INFORMED CONSENT TO FORENSIC EVALUATION: WHEN RETAINED BY DEFENSE AND STATE ENTITLED TO DISCOVERY

I, _____, have been informed by Doctor David Shapiro of the nature of this examination, namely an assessment of my mental status regarding the issue of (<u>competency to stand trial</u>), (<u>criminal responsibility</u>), (<u>sentencing</u>). I understand that Doctor Shapiro has been retained by my defense counsel and that the results of this evaluation can be obtained by the government's attorney. I understand that this is not a doctor-patient relationship bound by the traditional rules of confidentiality. I understand that Doctor Shapiro will be preparing a report and that copies of this report will go to my attorney and may be available to the government's attorney.

_____
Date

_____
Signature

_____
Witness

DAVID L. SHAPIRO, PhD
DIPLOMATE IN FORENSIC PSYCHOLOGY
AMERICAN BOARD OF PROFESSIONAL PSYCHOLOGY
1498-M REISTERTOWN ROAD
MAIL BOX 274
BALTIMORE, MARYLAND 21208

Telephone: (410) 653-5673

INFORMED CONSENT TO FORENSIC EVALUATION: COURT ORDERED

I, _____, have been informed by Doctor David Shapiro of the nature of this examination, namely an assessment of my mental status regarding the issue of (<u>competency to stand trial</u>), (<u>criminal responsibility</u>), (<u>sentencing</u>). Doctor Shapiro has informed me that his services have been requested and authorized by Judge _____ of the _____ Court. I understand that this is not a doctor-patient relationship bound by the traditional rules of confidentiality. Since this evaluation has been ordered by the Court, it is my understanding that copies of Doctor Shapiro's evaluation will be made available to my defense attorney, to the government attorney and to the Court.

_____   _____
Date   Signature

_____
Witness

DAVID L. SHAPIRO, PHD
DIPLOMATE IN FORENSIC PSYCHOLOGY
AMERICAN BOARD OF PROFESSIONAL PSYCHOLOGY
1498-M REISTERTOWN ROAD
MAIL BOX 274
BALTIMORE, MARYLAND 21208

Telephone: (410) 653-5673

INFORMED CONSENT TO FORENSIC EVALUATION: WHEN RETAINED BY PROSECUTION

I, _____, have been informed by Doctor David Shapiro of the nature of this examination, namely an assessment of my mental status regarding the issue of (<u>competency to stand trial</u>), (<u>criminal responsibility</u>), (<u>sentencing</u>). Doctor Shapiro has informed me that he has been retained by the prosecuting attorney to conduct an independent evaluation. I understand that this is not a doctor-patient relationship bound by the traditional rules of confidentiality. I understand that Doctor Shapiro will be preparing a report for the government attorney and that a copy of this report will be made available to my attorney.

_____
Date

_____
Signature

_____
Witness

APPENDIX D

Forensic Evaluation Outline

FORENSIC EVALUATION OUTLINE

NAME:		D.O.B.:	AGE:
PLACE OF BIRTH:	BIRTH ORDER:	RELIGION:	
PRESENT LIVING ARRANGEMENT:			
MARITAL STATUS:	OCCUPATION:	RACE:	
CHARGES:			

DOCUMENTS REVIEWED AND PEOPLE INTERVIEWED:

CONFIDENTIALITY WAIVER:

(State understanding in client's own words)

STATEMENT OF FACTS:

(Obtain from police reports, witness statements, interviews of police officers and witnesses, results of drug/alcohol screening, if available)

PATIENT'S VERSION OF OFFENSE:

(Include patient's perceptions, drug or alcohol usage at time, symptoms indicative of mental disorder; Patient's behavior at time of offense as related by family, friends, etc.; Relevant history leading to offense)

BEHAVIOR IN JAIL:

(Include patient's statements and interviews of correctional personnel)

JAIL PSYCHIATRIC RECORDS:

(Include discussion of consultations, medication, diagnosis, consistency or inconsistency with above behavior)

MENTAL STATUS EXAMINATION:

Appearance:

Behavior:

Orientation:

Attention:

Perception:

Memory:

Affect:

Speech:

Delusions:

Hallucinations:

Suicidal Ideation:

Judgment:

Indications of Toxicity:

Estimated Intelligence: *(If WAIS-III not given)*

Insight:

SOCIAL HISTORY:

(Obtain from patient and include that obtained from family/friends)

Early Childhood: *(Include family composition, nature of interactions, intactness, major events, illnesses, injuries, etc.)*

Latency: *(Include school performance, attitude toward studies, outside interests, nature of peer interaction)*

SOCIAL HISTORY: (continued)

    <u>Adolescence</u>: *(Include sexual development, identity issues, drugs, alcohol, nature of peer interaction, occupations)*

    <u>Young Adulthood</u>: *(Nature of interpersonal relationships, quality of job history)*

    <u>Adulthood</u>:

SOCIAL HISTORY: (continued)

Sexual and Marital: *(Dating, number of marriages, personality of spouse, reasons for separation, if any)*

Education: *(Include type of schools, grades, extracurricular activities)*

Vocational: *(Number of jobs, length)*

SOCIAL HISTORY: (continued)

Military: *(Include branch, dates, rank obtained, disciplinary actions, if any)*

Religious History:

Drug and Alcohol Abuse: *(Include history, kinds, extent, effect on behavior)*

CRIMINAL HISTORY:

Date	Place	Charge(s)	Disposition

PSYCHIATRIC HISTORY:

(Include nature of admissions, voluntary or involuntary, willingness to sign releases, type of treatment)

A.   <u>Family</u>:

B.   <u>Self</u>:

<u>CONSENT FOR DISCLOSURE OF RECORDS</u>

Client Name: _____   Client Number: _____

I hereby authorize _____
(name/title of person/agency)

_____
(complete address, including zip code)

to release information in my record to _____
(name/title of person/agency)

_____
(complete address, including zip code)

the following information:

       ☐ School Records
       ☐ Treatment Records
       ☐ Military Records
       ☐ Legal Records
       ☐ Psychological Testing (raw data)
       ☐ Other _____

The purpose or need for the disclosure is as follows: _____

_____

This consent is signed on the _____ day of _____, _____.

_____   _____
(Signature of client or person   **(Relationship of person authorized**
authorized to sign in lieu of   **to sign if not client)**
client)

_____
(Witness)

NEUROLOGICAL HISTORY:

A.   **Head Injuries and Sequelae**: *(Include hospitals where treatment rendered; Obtain records later)*

B.   **Blackouts**: *(Unrelated to drugs or alcohol)*

C.   **Dizzy Spells**:

D.   **Seizures**:

E.   **Stupor or Staring (Absence)**:

F.   **Repetitive, Stereotyped Movements**:

G.   **Micropsia, Macropsia, Distancing, Chromatopsia and so on**:

H.   **Pathological Intoxication**:

I.   **Spatial Disorientation**:

J.   **Learning Disabilities**:

NEUROLOGICAL HISTORY: (continued)

K.   Explosive Behavioral Outbursts - Minimal Provocation - Amnesia - Auras? - Peculiar Tastes or Smells:

L.   Confusional Episodes and/or Slurred Speech Unrelated to Drugs or Alcohol:

M.   Hallucinations Unrelated to Functional Mental Disorder:

N.   Fugue States:

O.   Déjà Vu:

P.   Jamais Vu:

Q.   Depersonalization, Derealization:

R.   Double Vision, Blurriness:

S.   History of Delirium Tremens:

T.   Memory Disturbances:

NEUROLOGICAL HISTORY: (continued)

U.   **Difficulty Understanding What You Read:**

V.   **Difficulty Following Conversations:**

W.   **Contact With Chemicals:**

X.   **History of Venereal Disease (Syphilis):**

CHRONOLOGICAL REVIEW OF PSYCHIATRIC RECORDS:

INTERVIEWS WITH TREATING THERAPISTS:

REVIEW OF GENERAL MEDICAL RECORDS:

(Check especially for head trauma, antianxiety or antidepressant medication)

REVIEW OF SCHOOL RECORDS:

REVIEW OF OCCUPATIONAL RECORDS:

REVIEW AND CRITIQUE OF PRIOR EVALUATIONS IN CURRENT CASE:

REFERRALS TO OTHER CONSULTANTS AND RESULTS OF THEIR EXAMINATIONS:

TEST RESULTS:

(Include test-taking attitude, behavior, degree of defensiveness, validity, motivation, reaction time, perseveration)

<u>**WAIS-III (or WISC-III)**</u>**:**

<u>**WMS-III**</u>**:**

TEST RESULTS: (continued)

<u>**Projectives**</u>:

<u>**Objective Personality Tests**</u>:

<u>**Neuropsychological Screening**</u>:

<u>**Neuropsychological Battery**</u>:

TEST RESULTS: (continued)

Malingering:

SUMMARY:

OPINION ON CRIMINAL RESPONSIBILITY (OR COMPETENCY):

(Specify how mental disorder may affect each functional capacity)

Competency:

Factual Understanding:

Rational Understanding:

Relation to Attorney:

Knowledge of Roles of Various People:

Knowledge of Pleas and Outcomes:

OPINION ON CRIMINAL RESPONSIBILITY (OR COMPETENCY): (continued)

Criminal Responsibility:

Mental Disorder - In What Way Does It Affect:

1) Ability to appreciate wrongfulness of behavior

2) Ability to conform to law (if applicable)

Other Forensic Issues (e.g., ability to waive Miranda Rights, competency to confess, whether or not the mental disorder resulted in an inability to form specific intent, etc.):

(Each issue: How does mental disorder relate to each of the functional capacities?)

RECOMMENDATIONS FOR DISPOSITION:

APPENDIX E

<u>Sample Reports</u>

DAVID L. SHAPIRO, PHD
DIPLOMATE IN FORENSIC PSYCHOLOGY
AMERICAN BOARD OF PROFESSIONAL PSYCHOLOGY
1498-M REISTERTOWN ROAD
MAIL BOX 274
BALTIMORE, MARYLAND 21208

Telephone: (410) 653-5673

February 2, 1998

Sally Sanders
Assistant United States Attorney
Office of the United States Attorney
555 Fourth Street, N.W.
Washington, DC 20001

Re: Robert Jones

Dear Ms. Sanders:

Pursuant to your referral, I have completed a psychological evaluation of Mr. Robert Jones, whom I saw at the District of Columbia Detention Center on January 24, 1998. In addition to clinical interview, I administered the Minnesota Multiphasic Personality Inventory. Also, on January 28, 1998 and January 31, 1998, I interviewed by telephone Secret Service Agent Oren Barton, who provided me with his observations of Mr. Jones' behavior at the time that the Secret Service questioned him.

Prior to my seeing Mr. Jones, I also reviewed extensive documents which not only you had provided but defense counsel, Ms. Ann Jenkins, had provided. Much of the material from Ms. Jenkins represented a series of highly delusional letters that Mr. Jones and his friend, Ms. Dorothy Carter, had sent to various officials, including the President of the United States.

During the course of the evaluation, Mr. Jones was very cooperative and subdued but quite willing to discuss the charges against him and what he perceived as the tortures that had been inflicted on him over the course of several years.

Mr. Jones was informed of the fact that I had been retained by the United States Attorney's Office, that there was no confidentiality in the interview and that reports would be sent to the U.S. Attorney and to his lawyer. He understood this and consented to the examination.

In fact, his opening words were "They tortured me." He spoke about people, who belonged to various fraternal orders, having machines that could send sound waves that kept him and his friend, Ms. Carter, in

Page 2
February 2, 1998

To: Sally Sanders
       Office of the United States Attorney
Re: Robert Jones

constant pain. He stated that they had been around for "a long time." He spoke about a biblical sect called Midians, who he said were also affiliated with the Masons and currently with the Ku Klux Klan. He spoke about the pain "in my nervous system," describing the pain as being in his spine and brain, and that he would experience vibrations in certain areas of his body which would also feel "heated up." He stated that these vibrations caused by the machines would make him impotent and he had "figured out" that this was due to the machines in 1984.

However, he noted that the tortures had really been going on "all the way back to my childhood," in which he described himself as always sickly, suffering from asthma and high fevers, and, in his teenage years, migraine headaches. He stated that he now realizes that these people had targeted him all his life. "They were after me ever since I was a child." He stated that they were assigned to him, though he does not know why. He figured out also that the tortures had been assigned to his family because "the machines affected everyone in my family and I see it now." He related his mother's high blood pressure, and her kidney problems, as well as his sister's failed marriage, to "the machines." He stated that in 1984 he went to see a Doctor Dalton, a psychologist in Saint Louis, Missouri, and noted that Doctor Dalton had an investigator, who found eyewitnesses who confessed to the Masons, Midians and Ku Klux Klan having the secret chambers, where the tortures took place. Mr. Jones indicated that the investigator had taken him and Ms. Carter to the eyewitness and the eyewitness told them about the chambers and the machines. He stated that at that point, "we realized what was happening to us." He spoke about Ms. Carter's difficulty being with mobility, fatigue and pains, and his, of course, as noted above, with the vibrations affecting his sexual function.

He was able to discuss his charge, "a gun violation," and stated that while he was aware of the fact that as a previously convicted felon he was not supposed to possess firearms, "I did not want to come to Washington, DC without protection." He stated that he had no intention of harming anyone, that he had come to the White House to seek help from President Clinton, who, because of a form letter which the White House had sent to him, he was convinced would be able to help him. He stated that he needed the guns in order to protect himself all across the country from the evil forces that were conspiring against him. He stated that he was not going to take chances and that the situation has not been corrected yet. He stated that his pain was so intense that he felt that it was worth violating the conditions of his parole in order to protect himself.

Page 3
February 2, 1998

To: Sally Sanders
        Office of the United States Attorney
Re: Robert Jones

He stated that he and Ms. Carter did not know how long they were going to stay in Washington and that they were unaware of rules in Washington, DC against the carrying of handguns.

He stated that they came to Washington because "if in any way we could get to Congress," Washington, DC would be the place. He cited the form letter from President Clinton as indicating that "he knew what we were saying because of our letter," referring to the long rambling letter that he and Ms. Carter had sent to the President. He was convinced that, because of this letter, they would have a chance of being heard if they came to Washington, DC. He stated that they visited the Justice Department and that prior to their coming to Washington, DC, they had actually spoken with a woman in the Justice Department on the telephone every three days. He stated that she understood that Mr. Jones and Ms. Carter had nowhere to stay and that they had provided their manuscript to her and "the Justice Department studied it." He indicated that the Justice Department wanted medical statements from both of them to verify what had happened to them. They also indicated that they had gone to the Mayor's Office to set up an appointment.

When I asked Mr. Jones why they went to the White House, he indicated that Ms. Carter did not feel that their trips to other places were working and that therefore they needed to "go to the top." He indicated that they had also planned to go to the Black Entertainment Network and had set up an appointment with a commentator on the Black Entertainment Network who has a program called Black Forum. He stated that the White House thing "just happened" and was reflective of Ms. Carter's sense of frustration.

He stated that since he has been in the jail, he has been treated with the antipsychotic medication, Risperdal, and that it does help him to sleep, though it does not make the pain engendered by the machines go away.

He indicated that his only adult incarceration was the twenty-year-old charge of armed robbery, for which he served a five year prison term.

He indicated that he had been hospitalized at the Veterans Administration Hospital in Columbia, Missouri in 1972 for two weeks, having checked himself in "following a bad acid trip." He said that at that time he was experiencing visual hallucinations which he felt were due to the drug but "I now realize they were due to the machines." He stated

To: Sally Sanders
          Office of the United States Attorney
Re: Robert Jones

that he did not tell anyone at the V.A. about the machines, believing that the symptoms were, in fact, caused by the drugs.

He denied any significant history of head trauma, though he did note one period of loss of consciousness in 1992. He stated that this was described as due to his drinking but he insisted that he was not drinking at the time but it was rather "due to the machine."

He described a basically unremarkable family history, though there was some obvious dysfunction, with his father leaving the family when Mr. Jones was very young and his having four stepfathers. He described a close relationship between himself, his mother and his sister, though he stated that growing up was "tough financially." He stated that he did well in school, graduated from high school and, in fact, had 1 ½ years of college courses while in prison in Missouri. He described no major family problems, stated that he had many friends in school and reported essentially an uneventful period of time in military service between 1968 and 1970.

I interviewed Secret Service Agent Oren Barton on January 28, 1998. Agent Barton stated that he felt that Mr. Jones was delusional, and spoke about the fact that Mr. Jones had told him that he was being followed by the Klan and that he wanted protection against their following him. Agent Barton also spoke about the fact that Mr. Jones spoke about the other groups, mainly the Masons and the Midians, and he stated that Mr. Jones told him that the Klan had been writing to them and following them. Agent Barton recalled that Mr. Jones talked about "the machines being turned up to cause more pain to them." He recalled Mr. Jones telling him that they came to Washington so that the President could help them to "stop the pains." Agent Barton's belief was that both Mr. Jones and Ms. Carter were no threat to the President and, in fact, he described them as "harmless crazy." He stated that he was convinced that they were being truthful when they spoke about the guns being protection against the Ku Klux Klan.

The Minnesota Multiphasic Personality Inventory reveals a valid profile, though, of some significance is the fact that he tended to deny a great deal of material. This is, of course, the total opposite of someone who is attempting to feign or malinger a mental disorder. In fact, despite being extremely guarded and denying, he made a variety of atypical and rarely given responses, and such defensiveness generally covers over psychotic processes.

To: Sally Sanders
         Office of the United States Attorney
Re: Robert Jones

There were no indications of any attempt to "fake sick" on the testing.

With these validity constraints in mind, that is, if anything, the test profile tends to underestimate the degree of mental illness, the pattern is indicative of a moderate to severe level of emotional instability. While overcontrolled much of the time, Mr. Jones is likely to have transitory episodes in which he would be seen as impatient and narcissistic with a moodiness that would vary from excitable to sullen.

Some of the patients rigidly overcontrol hostility for long periods of time, until it erupts in explosive episodes, but of some significance is the fact that these episodes appear to occur exclusively within a family setting. They do not appear to extend outside the family, as a general rule, for people with this kind of profile. At the same time, the hostility at times could suddenly be turned inward, such as a dramatic and serious suicide attempt.

The current level of organization of his day-to-day functioning is quite uneven. The profile is suggestive of a frankly paranoid schizophrenic psychosis, characterized by overt projections, chronic suspicions and intense jealousies. Of some note, the patients with such profiles showed relatively little breakdown of reality testing or disorganization of behavior, with the exception of the encapsulated delusional thinking. Patients with this profile attempt to maintain rigid controls and play strictly correct social roles. The responses also are consistent with Mr. Jones' complaints of a variety of physical ailments which are largely transitory hysterical conversion symptoms. Patients with such profiles strongly overreact to tangible organic illnesses.

Typical diagnoses with these patterns are of paranoid states and more chronic paranoid psychosis. That is, the profile is highly suggestive of extensive delusional thinking without the more wide-ranging thought disorganization that would be seen in a schizophrenic disorder. Some of these patients also present depressive trends, along with emotionally explosive (i.e., borderline) personality disorders.

The profile is also suggestive of a mild suicide risk, though the degree of risk is especially hard to evaluate because suicide attempts of these patients are so abrupt, situational and unplanned. There is also, with this pattern, a severe risk of chronic invalidism on the basis of the somatic complaints and this is also consistent with Mr. Jones' history.

Page 6
February 2, 1998

To: Sally Sanders
        Office of the United States Attorney
Re: Robert Jones

In summary, then, I would concur with the diagnosis reached earlier by Doctor Lewis of Mr. Jones, namely of a Delusional Disorder, Persecutory Type. Not only is this diagnosis consistent with the manner in which Mr. Jones presents himself but it is also totally consistent with the results of the Minnesota Multiphasic Personality Inventory.

Of course, the fact that Mr. Jones and Ms. Carter share this also leads to the diagnosis of the rare condition called Folie á Deux.

Based on these observations and the insistence by Mr. Jones on the fact that he had to carry his weapons in order to protect himself against the evil forces that were conspiring against him and the fact that he felt that his need for protection was significant enough to overcome his awareness that as a previously convicted felon he was not supposed to be carrying firearms, it is my opinion that Mr. Jones has established the fact that he did suffer from a severe mental disorder on June 14, 1997 such that he lacked the capacity to appreciate the wrongfulness of his behavior.

I trust the above analysis is of some assistance to you. Please feel free to call on me if you need further information.

Very truly yours,

David L. Shapiro, PhD
Diplomate in Forensic Psychology
American Board of Professional
        Psychology

DLS:esp

DAVID L. SHAPIRO, PHD
DIPLOMATE IN FORENSIC PSYCHOLOGY
AMERICAN BOARD OF PROFESSIONAL PSYCHOLOGY
1498-M REISTERTOWN ROAD
MAIL BOX 274
BALTIMORE, MARYLAND 21208

Telephone: (410) 653-5673

April 19, 1998

Martin Ryan, Esquire
Assistant United States Attorney
Office of the United States Attorney
  for the District of Columbia
District of Columbia Courthouse
500 Indiana Avenue, N.W.
Washington, DC 20001

Re: Robert Nash

Dear Mr. Ryan:

Pursuant to your request, I examined Mr. Robert Nash at the District of Columbia Jail on three separate occasions, March 7, 1998; March 19, 1998 and April 4, 1998, for a total of seven hours of clinical interview and psychological testing. The psychological testing included the Rorschach, the Minnesota Multiphasic Personality Inventory, the Projective Drawings, the Wechsler Adult Intelligence Scale, Revised Form, the Trailmaking Test (Halstead Battery), the Graham-Kendall Memory for Designs Test and the Luria Nebraska Neuropsychological Battery. In addition, I interviewed all of the bank tellers who were witnesses to the bank robberies with which Mr. Nash is charged, as well as Mr. Harold Martin, the man with whom Mr. Nash was living at the time of the robberies, and Ms. Vera Jones, Mr. Nash's former girlfriend, with whom he had broken up approximately three months prior to the first bank robbery. I also interviewed Detective William Sanders, the arresting officer in this case. In addition, I reviewed a variety of records which you had provided for me, including the military records and his hospitalization at the United States Naval Hospital in San Diego, the complete records from the Forensic Psychiatry Office, including the consultations at the D.C. Jail, as well as his inpatient record from the Forensic Center, reports from Robert Dawes, MD, Thomas Gardner, MD, Richard Carlson, MD and Patricia Bellows, PhD, all of whom had examined Mr. Nash on various occasions. Finally, I reviewed the statement which Mr. Nash had made to the police at the time of his arrest. Mr. Nash was informed of the nonconfidential nature of the evaluation, that I was retained by the United States Attorney and that I would be preparing a report which his attorney and the United States Attorney would get. He understood this and consented to the examination.

Page 2
April 19, 1998

To: Martin Ryan, Esquire
Re: Robert Nash

As you know, Mr. Nash is charged with a number of bank robberies occurring between April 12, 1997 and May 24, 1997. He apparently
robbed at least two banks on two separate occasions.

According to an interview with the arresting officer, Detective
William Sanders, Mr. Nash's approach to the bank robberies was consistent on each occasion. He would go into the bank with a note and a paper
bag, would get in line, would wait his turn and then hand a note to the
teller. The note would generally state that he had a gun and that the teller
should not go for the alarm. Detective Sanders indicated that, from his
observations of Mr. Nash at the time of the arrest, he did not appear to be
either intoxicated or high on drugs and he appeared to be neatly dressed
in what Detective Sanders described as a three-piece suit. He indicated
that at the time of arrest, Mr. Nash made no statements but did fill out his
rights statements, stating that he knew what his rights were. According
to Detective Sanders, Mr. Nash appeared logical, rational, totally aware
of what he had done and of the questions being asked. Detective Sanders
was specifically asked whether or not he had had any contact with psychiatric patients and he responded affirmatively, stating that he had had
opportunity to arrest many individuals who were either on elopement from
Saint Elizabeth's Hospital or were outpatients. He indicated that Mr. Nash
did not in any way appear similar to the seriously disturbed individuals
with whom he, Detective Sanders, has had contact.

Interview with the various bank tellers indicated basically the
same perceptions that Detective Sanders had.

Ms. Ann Tolan, a teller at the District of Columbia National Bank,
described Mr. Nash as smooth and confident, blending into the public.
She stated that he was dressed in an average manner and stated that he
handed her a note stating, "If you love life, put the money in the bag."
She indicated that her head teller came up and Mr. Nash told her not to
talk to her. She indicated that he did not slur his speech, did not seem
high or intoxicated and "seemed very confident and very cool." She stated
that he did not appear preoccupied and maintained good eye contact with
her.

Interview with Ms. Jennifer Pauley, another teller at the District
of Columbia National Bank, indicated that Mr. Nash also handed her a
note telling her to put the money in the bag. She indicated that Mr. Nash
"directed me and pointed to the twenties and tens," telling her not to put
one-dollar bills in the bag. She stated that he told her, "Don't say anything, or pull any buttons." She stated that when he initially left, he had
left the hold-up note behind him, and then came back and got the note

To: Martin Ryan, Esquire
Re: Robert Nash

from her. She described him as calm, neatly dressed, not appearing bizarre in any manner. Again, she described no slurring of speech, no intoxication and no apparent preoccupations. She stated that he did not talk to himself or, for that matter, to anyone else. She stated that he had his hand wrapped in a newspaper and she, Ms. Pauley, did not know whether or not he had a gun in the newspaper.

Interview with Ms. Carmen Beal, a supervisor at the District of Columbia National Bank, revealed the impression that she saw Mr. Nash passing one of the tellers a paper bag and that "he never stopped looking at her hands." Again, she stated that there was nothing peculiar about him, that he did not appear intoxicated or high, there was no slurring to his speech and that he was wearing a hat.

Interview with Ms. Dorothy Varga revealed the impression that Mr. Nash walked up and had a bouquet of flowers wrapped in a paper. When she called him over to where she was standing, he passed her a note and she recalls fainting from fright. She was then told that Mr. Nash had looked at her and walked out of the bank.

Ms. Carol Barton, a teller at the American Security Bank, indicated that Mr. Nash had come up to her window and handed her a note stating, "If you love life, give me your money." He then stated, "Hurry up or I'll kill you." She described him as being dressed nicely, in clean clothes, manifesting nothing unusual in his speech, no slurring and that he seemed totally coherent. She stated that he had a strong, forceful, commanding voice and did not appear to be responding to any imaginary forces. She described him as stable, steady and not preoccupied.

Finally, an interview with Ms. Enid Dawkins indicated that Mr. Nash had walked to her window, had waited for her to finish talking to another teller and produced a notebook which she described as a spiral binder, and once again presented the note to her, "If you enjoy life, fill this bag." She indicated once again that he asked for twenties, tens and fives, and walked out in a calm manner. Again, she described no evidence of preoccupation on his part.

On March 21, 1998, I interviewed Mr. Harold Martin, a man with whom Mr. Nash was living at the time of the bank robberies. Mr. Martin indicated that Mr. Nash used to be an employee of his and prior to that time they were "just friends." He described Mr. Nash as "a nice person" and proceeded to talk about the fact that Mr. Nash had recently broken up with Ms. Jones, and that he was "broken up over it." He described Mr. Nash as quite depressed, and on a few occasions seemed preoccupied

Page 4
April 19, 1998

To: Martin Ryan, Esquire
Re: Robert Nash

and distant, "mumbling to himself." He indicated that Mr. Nash never described experiencing auditory hallucinations and "never seemed out of touch." On one occasion, Mr. Martin stated that he had seen Mr. Nash shaving his head with a razor during the months that the bank robberies occurred. Mr. Martin indicated that this behavior seemed strange to him and when he inquired of Mr. Nash why he was doing this, he indicated that Mr. Nash told him that he was seeking "a new appearance." Mr. Martin stated that on a few occasions he would see Mr. Nash staring at the walls, but that he would never describe what was going on when he appeared to be mumbling to himself.

Interview with Ms. Vera Jones, Mr. Nash's former girlfriend, revealed the impression that Mr. Nash was "a nice guy, but weird." She indicated that he seemed obsessed with darkness and that he would go into a dark room, sit and talk to himself. She indicated that Mr. Nash was extremely jealous, "unnaturally jealous," and would become very upset if Ms. Jones even talked to another man. She described him as getting violent in these jealous rages, and "grabbing at my neck." She indicated that on one occasion, when they were having difficulties and were sleeping in separate rooms, Mr. Nash drilled a hole in her wall so that he could spy on her and make sure she was not involved in sexual liaisons with anyone else. She stated that when Mr. Nash would get high, "he would look crazy," but she would not describe exactly what this involved. She could only describe it as "a different atmosphere about him." She indicated that he never appeared to manifest any symptoms of hallucinations. She did infer that there were a number of sexual difficulties between the two of them, but stated she preferred not to discuss them.

Review of Mr. Nash's naval records reveals that he was admitted to the United States Naval Hospital in San Diego, California on September 16, 1986, stating, "I am on the verge of insanity." The admitting impression of the examiner was that he was emotionally immature and demanding. Mental status was within normal limits, though it was noted that his judgment was poor, impulsive and immature. There was no clinical evidence, according to the examiner, of delusions, hallucinations, inappropriate affect, impaired reality testing, thought disorder or an organic brain syndrome. It was noted that there were a number of disciplinary actions previously when Mr. Nash was away from duty. While hospitalized, he was described as showing angry emotional outbursts when he did not get his way, but still no evidence of psychosis, depression or severe neurosis. Discharge was recommended based on the fact that Mr. Nash could not adjust to military life. The final diagnosis was of emotional instability. It should be noted that prior to this hospitalization, while still serving on the aircraft carrier, Kitty Hawk, Mr. Nash had reported hallucinations, stating

Page 5
April 19, 1998

To: Martin Ryan, Esquire
Re: Robert Nash

that "an invisible thing is after me," and later on, was described as being hyperactive and showing a flight of ideas. It was suspected that Mr. Nash had gotten high on "Red Devils," though he denied this to the examining physician. He also described difficulties in sleeping, and a preliminary diagnosis at that point was of schizoid personality.

Following his arrest on these charges, Mr. Nash made a suicidal gesture at the District of Columbia Jail, and was examined by Doctor Raskin of the Forensic Psychiatry Office, who described him as depressed and suicidal, and recommended transfer to the forensic facility.

He was transferred to the forensic facility shortly thereafter, and while there was examined on three separate occasions by Richard Carlson, MD. In his first report, Doctor Carlson made reference to Mr. Nash's drug-induced hallucinosis in the Navy and his heavy drug abuse prior to his arrest. He noted no evidence of disorganized thinking, bizarre behavior, anxiety or depression and no evidence of such behavior on the forensic unit from June 2 to August 1, 1997. Nevertheless, Mr. Nash would complain of depression and hallucinations, though he would manifest no outward signs of that according to the hospital staff. At that point, Doctor Carlson diagnosed Mr. Nash as suffering from a drug-induced psychosis, that he was regarded as responsible for his criminal activity under the law, but that there was question about his competency.

In Doctor Carlson's second evaluation, he again made reference to Mr. Nash's "self-reports of every imaginable symptom," but no observable evidence of these symptoms. The question continued, in Doctor Carlson's mind, of the genuineness of Mr. Nash's symptomatology, but he entertained the possibility that Mr. Nash was suffering from a Ganser Syndrome and requested a continuance once again.

In Doctor Carlson's final report to the Court, he again noted that Mr. Nash continued to complain of command hallucinations, but there was no evidence of disorganization of thinking and behavior. Doctor Carlson did note, however, that continued observation revealed that there was evidence of mental illness, but that most likely it was not schizophrenia. He noted that when Mr. Nash was taken off medication he became paranoid and aggressive, and psychological testing did definitely reveal disorganization of thinking. Doctor Carlson's final diagnosis was that Mr. Nash was suffering from a drug-induced hallucinatory disorder, but maintained his opinion that since it was due to the voluntary ingestion of drugs, Mr. Nash should be regarded as criminally responsible. During the course of his hospitalization at the Forensic Center, he was examined by Doctor

Page 6
April 19, 1998

To: Martin Ryan, Esquire
Re: Robert Nash

Patricia Bellows, a staff psychologist. She noted that Mr. Nash was quite curious about the purpose of the tests and how they would be used.

Her administration of the Wechsler Adult Intelligence Scale-Revised Form to Mr. Nash revealed no evidence of autistic logic or peculiar verbalizations, and no indications of a schizophrenic thought disorder. However, she did comment on the scatter among Mr. Nash's subtest scaled scores, suggesting the emotional interference with his thinking that would be consistent with an underlying thought disorder. The Minnesota Multiphasic Personality Inventory revealed a high F scale and elevation of all of his clinical scales, which suggested the possibility of malingering. However, since the Rorschach Test revealed impairment in reality testing, a deterioration in the ability to censor sexual content, as well as evidence of loose thinking and autistic logic, coupled with brittle defenses which did not hold up well when the patient was anxious, the conclusion was that there was a genuine underlying disorder. There was also a question raised as to the possibility of an organic brain syndrome, especially due to some deficits in short-term memory.

While at the Forensic Center, Mr. Nash was treated initially with Thorazine, subsequently with Haldol, and finally with Loxitane.

During the course of his hospitalization, there was continual notation made of the discrepancy between the symptoms which Mr. Nash described and his overt ward behavior. For instance, notes in the chart revealed Mr. Nash's statement that voices told him that he belonged in a future time zone, but that there was no evidence of unusual behavior on the ward, and he was described as being in a stable emotional state. Again, ward notes revealed no evidence of his responding to auditory hallucinations, but the attending physician would note that he described instances typical of paranoid thinking, as well as auditory hallucinations. This, of course, was prior to the period of time when he was taken off medication and his behavior deteriorated.

During the period of time that Mr. Nash was hospitalized at the Forensic Center, he was seen by a number of outside psychiatrists who had varying opinions. He was seen by Doctor Thomas Gardner, who noted in his report a variety of unrelated symptoms, and it was Doctor Gardner's belief that Mr. Nash was malingering.

In a report by Doctor Robert Dawes, he noted that in his initial interview, Mr. Nash was paranoid, showed inappropriate affect, pressured speech and loose associations. He also noted from material describing family interviews that Mr. Nash had complained to his parents about

To: Martin Ryan, Esquire
Re: Robert Nash

auditory hallucinations when he was quite young and that at the age of sixteen, his mother took him to see a psychiatrist due to his seclusiveness and his "living in his own world." Doctor Dawes' conclusion was that Mr. Nash was genuinely mentally ill, diagnosed as schizo-affective schizophrenia and that he committed the bank robberies without regard to the likelihood of his apprehension. Doctor Dawes' opinion was in part based on Mr. Nash's deterioration when he was taken off medication, coupled with the results of Doctor Bellows' psychological testing.

Following Mr. Nash's return to jail, he was described as continually preoccupied with suicidal thoughts, hearing voices telling him to kill himself, and he continued to be treated with Thorazine in the jail.

Finally, it should be noted that in Mr. Nash's statement to the police, he made no mention of hallucinations being involved in any of his criminal activities, and in fact stated a very rational approach to the crime, indicating that he was out of work and "I would do anything to survive."

More recent medical records from the District of Columbia Jail described Mr. Nash as stable and coherent, though there was some evidence of anxiety and tension and continued complaints on Mr. Nash's part that he was experiencing hallucinations.

During the course of my interviews with Mr. Nash, he was consistently neatly dressed, cooperative and well-oriented. Attention, perception and memory were intact, his affect was notably depressed, but his speech was coherent. He manifested no evidence whatsoever of any paranoid ideation, but did speak freely about what he described as his hallucinations. He stated that he was regressing and that we was now hearing voices telling him to castrate himself. He indicated that this had been a hallucination which he had several years ago. He indicated that while he had frequently thought about suicide previously, he had not made any suicide attempts until one which resulted in his transfer to the Forensic Center. He stated that he was depressed for many years because he could not communicate the way he wanted to: "I was always an outsider." Mr. Nash said he did not go along with the way other people acted, and people treated him like an outsider, "like I was trying to start trouble." Mr. Nash admitted to periods of heavy drinking, at times that he was depressed, feeling that he had to "drink until I felt drunk." He denied ever experiencing delirium tremens, but did indicate that while in the Navy he had combined drinking and "Red Devils," and had passed out many times from the combination of the drug and alcohol. He indicated that he has experimented with virtually all drugs, but regularly uses marijuana. He stated that he has used LSD and PCP on a few occasions, but does not

To: Martin Ryan, Esquire
Re: Robert Nash

have any drug that he regards as his favorite. He described primarily pleasant hallucinations, which he described as "voices and visions" when taking drugs, but on one or two occasions stated that he had had "bad trips" characterized by visual hallucinations of insects and spiders.

Mr. Nash indicated on interview that he was charged with five bank robberies occurring between April and May of 1997. He stated that he was in a very depressed state of mind, was not eating or sleeping well and "had problems," which he described as the reexperiencing of the auditory hallucinations which he has had on and off all his life. He stated that he was out of work for approximately five months and was living with a friend of his, Harold Martin. He stated that the crime that he committed was totally against his personality, and he indicated that he had never been arrested before. He described previous auditory hallucinations as telling him that he was part of the miraculous conception and that the voices in the past had told him to castrate himself or someone else. He indicated that the voices would constantly tell him to castrate himself or someone else, as well as telling him that he was from another world and that he had to do things out of compulsion. When asked what these things were, he indicated that the voices would tell him to taste feces and spit out all the time. He indicated that he never did comply with these hallucinatory demands, but that he would, every two minutes, make the sign of the cross out of a compulsion. He also indicated a variety of compulsive rituals, such as checking that the door was closed eight or nine times, and checking whether the stove was off "a hundred times or more." He stated that earlier he had tried to psychoanalyze himself "like Freud."

At the times of the offense, he indicated that the voices told him to "get money" and "take money from the bank." He stated that these voices had "worked on my mind for a while, about three weeks." He stated that he went downtown, continuing to hallucinate, and was trying to decide whether to resist the voice or go along with it. He indicated that he was in this state of indecision for approximately four to five hours when he finally decided to go into the bank. He stated that he was trying to resist it, because "it was not my personality to do it." He indicated that the voices directing him toward antisocial activities were a change in his thinking and values and "I became a different person overnight." He stated that he did have thoughts about the fact that he would be breaking the law but "that thought was not as powerful as the others." He indicated that he recalled thinking about an alarm going off and the fact that he might get caught. In fact, he stated that he frequently had the feeling that he would get caught following the bank robberies.

To: Martin Ryan, Esquire
Re: Robert Nash

Mr. Nash indicated during interview that he had used drugs for a period of several months but was not using drugs at the time of the crime. He indicated that he had been using LSD, cocaine and alcohol and drinking heavily. He stated that the night before the offense he had used drugs and they had created in him a feeling of hypersensitivity, like "everything was going fast in me and everything else was in slow motion." He stated that this feeling of himself being speeded up, and the world being in slow motion, was going on at the times of the offense.

When asked what the impact of the drugs on the auditory hallucinations are, he indicated that they tend to make the voices less intense, but at the same time make him supersensitive to noise. He stated that while he had been drinking prior to the offense, he was not drunk at the times of the robberies themselves.

Mr. Nash indicated that he gave a statement to the police the morning following his arrest and that he was still experiencing auditory hallucinations at that point in time. He stated that his thoughts were jumbled, that he was not thinking straight. It is noteworthy, of course, upon reviewing his statement to the police, that there is no evidence of any incoherence nor any reference to auditory hallucinations.

Hallucinatory experiences were not consistent with the way in which he committed the robberies and the fact that he committed the robberies because "I've looked for work and was at the point that I would do just about anything to survive." He further indicated, "I tried to be very low key and to be polite with all the tellers. I didn't want anyone to get hurt, and I didn't want the tellers to be left emotionally scarred from the acts I did." Given the coherence of this statement, as well as the lack of any indication of ongoing hallucination, one must question the validity of Mr. Nash's statement that at the time of the confession to the police, "My thoughts were jumbled and I wasn't thinking straight."

Mr. Nash indicated that he made a suicide attempt while in jail "because of my personality change," and in fact had decided to kill himself even before he was arrested. He indicated that the fact he was caught and incarcerated was not the motive for his attempt at suicide. He stated that he went to the Forensic Center from June until November of 1997, at which point he was returned to the D.C. Jail where he has remained ever since. He spoke about the fact that Thorazine appears to aggravate his hallucinations, and that Haldol makes him "hyper and restless like I'm on speed." He stated that in January of 1998 he had again attempted suicide because of a thought that "I've made a mess of myself." He recalls thinking about the Japanese committing hara-kiri because they had brought dishonor on themselves, and he felt that he had done the same.

Mr. Nash described his hospitalization at the U.S. Naval Hospital in San Diego as due to hallucinations that he had experienced following his return from military service. He received a General Discharge Under Honorable Conditions.

Mr. Nash denies having had any serious head injuries, but did indicate that he has hit his head on many occasions and on at least one of these occasions had been rendered unconscious. He did report consistent headaches, especially migraine headaches, but denied blackouts, seizures or any symptoms of absence. Mr. Nash indicated that when he was younger, especially in his teen years, he had frequent episodes of micropsia and macropsia, but related these to a high fever that he had at the time. He stated that these recurred very recently, since he has been incarcerated, but, prior to that, stated he had not experienced them since his adolescence. He indicated that he has experiences of déjà vu and jamais vu approximately twice a month. He also stated that he had been told that he can get quite violent, and recalls only "things getting dark, when I get mad, and it seems like I pass out for a minute."

Mr. Nash was born in Trenton, New Jersey on February 21, 1967, the older of two siblings. He indicated that his parents have always been together, and that his father was a construction worker and his mother a government clerk. He stated that he had a close family and was generally closer to his mother, describing his father as a rather distant authority figure. He recalls arguments between his parents, but does not recall any evidence of physical abuse.

Mr. Nash indicated that he went as far as the eleventh grade in school, at which time he dropped out and joined the Navy, having lost interest in school. He stated that at this time his lack of interest in school was due primarily to his experiencing auditory hallucinations and "being in another world." He stated that his grades were generally mixed, having some very good grades and some quite poor. He described himself as a loner primarily, having only one friend, but usually playing by himself and "I enjoyed being by myself." He stated that he had no girlfriends because he was so shy, and was into "painting and science projects."

Mr. Nash stated that he served in the Navy for three years, saw many casualties while he was aboard ship and that when he returned to the United States, the voices had gotten progressively worse. He stated

To: Martin Ryan, Esquire
Re: Robert Nash

that following his discharge, he came home to the New Jersey area, heard about the Merchant Marines, joined them and served in the Merchant Marines for approximately four years.

He indicated that he was married for approximately four years, but kept his hallucinatory experiences to himself, "nobody knew about the voices." He described this as a rather unstable period in his life with no steady employment, but rather many short-term jobs. When asked why the marriage broke up, he stated, "She got into women's liberation," and felt that she had no life of her own.

He stated that he had some difficulties adjusting to his wife's leaving him, but following this "led a care-free life." He indicated that he was divorced from his wife in 1993, though he had been separated for several years prior to that. Following the separation from his wife, he stated that he became a correctional officer in a women's prison in New Jersey, a job that lasted for five years. He came to the Washington, DC area in 1991 and stated that since he was always interested in the arts, he would try to find work as an artist. However, he never succeeded in this and instead was only able to obtain a job as a house painter and as a chauffeur.

On the current battery of psychological tests, Mr. Nash achieves a verbal IQ of 80, a performance IQ of 84 and a resultant full-scale IQ of 84, placing him within the low-average range of intellectual functioning. There is extensive scatter on his subtest scaled scores, indicating a rather severe disruption of his intellectual functioning by underlying emotional problems, though there is no overt intrusion of pathological thinking processes into his cognitive functioning. Specifically, while general information and vocabulary skills remain intact, there is a marked decrement on his subtest measuring social judgment. Here he manifests himself as showing very poor judgment, in an oscillation between rather rigid defenses and impulsive acting-out. Specifically, this would tend to indicate that while he has the fund of information available to him, because of his underlying emotional problems, he is unable to apply such information adequately to the world around him. In addition to these problems in judgment and impulse control, there is a marked decrement in attention and concentration, as well as some peculiar variations in his ability to think abstractly.

In terms of performance skills, he experiences much difficulty on a task of visual concentration, being virtually unable to screen out irrelevant stimuli. In a similar manner, there is much difficulty in his ability to understand and appreciate the parameters of various social situations.

Page 12
April 19, 1998

To: Martin Ryan, Esquire
Re: Robert Nash

Finally, there is a good deal of variation in his ability to perform perceptual motor tasks.

In summary, most of the subtests of the Wechsler Adult Intelligence Scale show the intrusion of many emotional problems and, in fact, are highly consistent with the results obtained several months ago at the Forensic Center by Doctor Bellows.

The Projective testing reveals rather poor reality testing at present with much evidence of cognitive slippage. There are many indications of an underlying thought disorder, primarily in the manner in which he organizes the world around him. That is, when he is able to obsessively break down situations into minute details, he does not appear so disorganized. On the other hand, when he attempts to put "the pieces of the puzzle together," he frequently reaches rather unusual levels of reasoning. The specific factor which appears to precipitate the deterioration in thinking each time is his preoccupation with underlying sexual concerns. There are frequently intrusions of sexual ideation in an inappropriate manner into various other perceptions and much evidence of sexual confusion, resulting in the peculiar ways of perceiving reality noted above. This preoccupation with sexuality also causes much depression on his part, as well as some suggestions of paranoia. When affectively stimulated, these distortions become particularly notable and result in frankly autistic logic. At such times, his internal distortions totally determine the manner in which he reasons rather than external reality determining his thinking. Once he lapses into such thinking, he becomes exceedingly disorganized and shows virtually no ability to effectively organize the world around him. Consistent with this evidence of many disturbed percepts regarding sexuality is the sexual identity confusion noted in his Projective Drawings, coupled with rather poor impulse control and an attempt to distance himself intellectually from these conflicts.

Finally, on the Minnesota Multiphasic Personality Inventory, there is further indication of the underlying disturbance. He presents a valid profile, rather than a distorted profile which he presented at the forensic facility. Here, the profile is indicative of a rather severe disturbance, consistent with a thought disorder, confusion, poor memory and difficulty concentrating. Finally, while one of the screening tests for central nervous system impairment does reveal moderate impairment, this can largely be attributed to the difficulties in attention and concentration which Mr. Nash's emotional disturbance causes. The Graham-Kendall Memory for Designs Test, a screening test of perceptual motor tasks, is within the normal range, tending to rule out, at least in terms of the norms used for this test, the presence of any severe brain damage. Also, all of the clinical

To: Martin Ryan, Esquire
Re: Robert Nash

and summary scales of the Luria Nebraska Neuropsychological Battery are well below the patient's critical level.

In summary, then, the interview and test data do tend to suggest the presence of an underlying mental disorder but one which Mr. Nash at times appears to utilize, exaggerate and manipulate for his own ends. That is, the distortions in thinking and the consistent pattern of the impairment in attention and concentration noted on the testing are highly consistent with a rather pervasive mental disorder. I would certainly agree with Doctor Bellows that the subtle nature of many of these disturbances could not possibly be known to Mr. Nash and therefore this appears to be a valid demonstration of an underlying thought disorder. Nevertheless, Mr. Nash's attempt to utilize this underlying thought disorder to excuse his behavior at the time of the offense simply does not fit with the facts as they are noted. Specifically, as noted previously, despite Mr. Nash's descriptions of the overpowering influence of these hallucinations, none of the witnesses who observed Mr. Nash at the times of the offense, or shortly thereafter, noted any bizarre or unusual behavior. This is true not only in the perceptions of the bank tellers but also in the statement of the arresting officer, who indicated that he has had contact with many psychiatric patients in the past, nor is there any evidence of disturbance of thinking in the statement made to the police within twenty-four hours after his arrest, a time when Mr. Nash, himself, described his thoughts as being totally disorganized. In addition, the fact that Mr. Nash had a prewritten note at the times of the bank robberies, coupled with various statements that he made at the times of the offense, clearly indicates a recognition on his part of what was going on. Such statements are: "Don't say anything or pull any buttons," "I want to see your hands" and "Don't give me any funny money," indicating even his awareness of bait money.

Interview with Mr. Harold Martin also revealed a rather striking observation: Mr. Nash was shaving his head in order to get "a new appearance," in the midst of the bank robberies. This would again tend to indicate some sensitivity on Mr. Nash's part to the fact that he might have been identified and was trying to change his appearance.

Mr. Nash's own statements to the effect that he spent four or five hours deciding whether or not to resist the hallucinatory commands (if they even existed) clearly indicate a substantial degree of control over his actions regardless of what the underlying mental disorder was "forcing" him to do. In addition, Mr. Nash clearly indicated awareness of the wrongfulness of his behavior, not only in the statements noted above which he made to the bank tellers but in the fact that even in the present interview he thought about the fact that he was breaking the law, he

Page 14
April 19, 1998

To: Martin Ryan, Esquire
Re: Robert Nash

thought about an alarm being set off and he thought about getting caught. In addition, Mr. Nash describes himself, albeit inconsistently to different examiners, as being under the influence of drugs at the times of the offense. He would tell some people that he had taken drugs on the days of the offense and others that it had been in the days preceding the offense, but under any circumstances it would appear that the drug intoxication significantly influenced his behavior. Finally, and perhaps most critically, even if one accepts the description which Mr. Nash gave of various hallucinations, hallucinations by their very nature are related to areas of psychic distress in a given individual. Clearly, the psychological testing, as well as clinical evaluation from a variety of sources, pinpoint Mr. Nash's sexual identity as being a critical and perhaps the most central area of distress in his life. Even his former girlfriend, Ms. Jones, hints at the fact that this was an area of significant disturbance for Mr. Nash. Mr. Nash, himself, in his description of his earlier hallucinations which would tell him to castrate himself, suggested the importance of this particular area in his own emotional problems. Under such circumstances, it would be expected that were he experiencing hallucinations at the times of the offense, they would be sexually-related hallucinations rather than voices telling him to "rob banks." In short, what is perhaps most critical is that Mr. Nash attempts to account for his behavior by references to auditory hallucinations and this simply does not fit with the fact that his underlying disturbances are in the sexual area and that if he were experiencing "voices" at the time, they would almost certainly have these sexually-disturbing themes in them.

Therefore, in summary, it is my opinion that while there is evidence of a rather pervasive underlying mental disease, it does not appear to be connected in any way to the series of bank robberies which Mr. Nash committed. Mr. Nash most likely was experiencing some effects of drug intoxication but it is highly unlikely, in my opinion, that even this drug intoxication produced the auditory hallucinations which he alleges resulted in the bank robberies. In short, therefore, it is my opinion that while Mr. Nash does suffer from an underlying mental disorder, most likely a schizophrenic reaction, this did not, in any way, affect his behavior at the times of the alleged offense. In my opinion, despite the mental disorder, he was very much aware of the wrongfulness of his behavior and capable of confirming his behavior to the requirements of the law. The alleged offense, if committed by Mr. Nash, in my opinion was not the product of his underlying mental disease.

Page 15
April 19, 1998

To: Martin Ryan, Esquire
Re: Robert Nash

    I trust the above analysis is of some assistance to you. If I may be of further help, please do not hesitate to call on me.

Very truly yours,

David L. Shapiro, PhD
Diplomate in Forensic Psychology
American Board of Professional
    Psychology

DLS:esp

DAVID L. SHAPIRO, PhD
DIPLOMATE IN FORENSIC PSYCHOLOGY
AMERICAN BOARD OF PROFESSIONAL PSYCHOLOGY
1498-M REISTERTOWN ROAD
MAIL BOX 274
BALTIMORE, MARYLAND 21208

Telephone: (410) 653-5673

July 30, 1996

Frank Howard, Esquire
States Attorney of Howard County
New Courthouse
Ellicott City, MD 21043

Re: Richard Johnson

Dear Mr. Howard:

　　　Pursuant to your referral, I have completed a psychological evaluation of Mr. Richard Johnson, whom I saw on several occasions, both at the Howard County Detention Center and the Clifton T. Perkins Hospital Center, for clinical interview and for psychological testing. I saw Mr. Johnson on October 9, 1995; October 17, 1995; October 18, 1995; November 3, 1995; December 7, 1995; December 11, 1995; March 7, 1996 and May 14, 1996. In addition to clinical interview and history-taking, I administered the following psychological tests: Projective Drawings, Rorschach, a variety of neuropsychological screening tests, including the Stroop Color-Word Test, Trailmaking Test (Halstead Battery), Aphasia Screening Test, Graham-Kendall Memory for Designs Test, Hooper Visual Organization Test, Symbol Digit Modalities Test and the Booklet Categories Test. In addition, I administered the Wechsler Adult Intelligence Scale, Revised Form and the Minnesota Multiphasic Personality Inventory (MMPI-2). Also, I reviewed a large number of documents which you had provided for me, including a variety of Grand Jury testimony transcripts, transcripts of preliminary hearings, police reports, psychiatric records from the Howard County Detention Center, Mr. Johnson's personal diaries and a chronology of events. In addition, I interviewed a large number of family members, friends and acquaintances, including Ms. Wilma Shelton, Chief Psychologist at the Howard County Detention Center; Mrs. Helen Johnson, the defendant's mother; Mr. Walter Johnson, the defendant's father; Officer Robert Stanton, the officer who initially apprehended Mr. Johnson; Ms. Fara Colton, Mr. Johnson's older sister; Mr. Johnson's older brother, Stephen Johnson; Detective Lois Palmer; Mr. Johnson's older brother, George; a cousin of Mr. Johnson, David Williams; Cathy and John Sanders, two other cousins and several friends, including Mary Carson, Donna Nast, Lily Thompson and Sandra Towns. I was not able to interview Mr. Robert Rogers but consulted with Peter Raines, MD regarding his interview of Mr. Rogers.

Page 2
July 30, 1996

To: Frank Howard, Esquire
         States Attorney of Howard County
Re: Richard Johnson

As you know, Mr. Johnson is charged with the homicide of a close friend, Mr. Harold Barnes, whom he allegedly shot to death on July 1, 1995. Details of the offense are well-known to you and will not be repeated here.

Clinical Interviews:

Throughout the course of all of the interviews, Mr. Johnson was pleasant, cooperative, well-oriented and eager to present his perception of the events leading to the homicide. Mr. Johnson was informed about the limits of the confidentiality and was clearly able to understand this, indicating, "You will be reviewing all the information on the case, because I am taking an NGRI, and I have waived my right to confidentiality. You will be writing reports to the Court, and the prosecutor and my attorney will get copies of the reports."

Mr. Johnson mentioned that he is on the Psychiatric Unit at the Howard County Detention Center and was receiving the antipsychotic medication, Prolixin, 5 mg., twice daily. He noted that initially his vision was somewhat blurry and his hands shaky but those side effects have since disappeared. He indicated that he was going through "negative thoughts" which he described as "impressions of how people were spiritually connected to me," and frankly described, with a good deal of insight, his own paranoid feelings, impressions that people were trying to get to him sexually, thoughts that he could read people's spiritual thinking and that he would assume that things were happening which were not really occurring. He indicated that at the present time, that is at the time that I was examining him, he was "back to his normal self." He dated his psychotic deterioration to 1993, when he "rededicated myself to the church." There were clear ideas of reference as he described his religious readings, feeling that various stories were written about him. He felt that only a "spiritual man" could understand the "true spiritual messages" in these religious writings. He described himself as "a catalyst for rapture." He described very bizarre transformations of the alphabet and numbers which he stated would get the true spiritual insight and get people's true spirit. He stated that this was an internal language and that he never confronted people with it. He said that when he finally did mention it to some other people, "they thought I was tripping." He assumed people were saying things about him and described his difficulties in various jobs as a result of his paranoid thinking. He described a relationship with Lily Thompson and subsequently with Mary Carson and the onset of some delusional ideas that "I thought everyone around me was trying to

To: Frank Howard, Esquire
         States Attorney of Howard County
Re: Richard Johnson

achieve things sexually." He demonstrated a highly idiosyncratic interpretation of events which appeared to become more profound between the Fall of 1994 and the Winter of 1995. He became very distrustful of his friends, thinking that they were doing things behind his back, and at this point he walked off his job and withdrew from graduate school in March of 1995. He also noted that his mother had moved back to Baltimore in February of 1995. Mr. Johnson noted that his parents had been separated for fifteen years, that they had gotten back together and that his mother had gone to New York to be with his father, and he was living by himself in his mother's home in southwest Baltimore. Mary had moved in with him, but when his mother returned, Mary had to move out. He described a number of conflicts with his mother at that point in time and spoke about how a variety of bizarre sexual thoughts kept interfering with his work. He described himself as becoming progressively more depressed and "I started relating spirituality and time," where the hour would represent a group where he saw someone else doing something, the minute would refer to the number of men who were performing a spiritual gift and that this spiritual gift was having sex with these various people. He described himself as progressively withdrawing from people more and more and that he would have to drive to different cities in order to pick up spiritual trains that other people had left behind. Notably, as he described this, even in his current state of remission, his thoughts became very bizarre and disorganized.

He described the incidents leading up to the shooting as stemming from a period of deep depression in June of 1995. He indicated that the woman with whom he was involved at that time, Donna, "saw my depression and tried to help but I shut her out." He indicated that she was driving a rented car and that he told her that he needed the car to go to a political meeting. However, he never went to the meeting and took Donna's car in order to go "on a spiritual journey," feeling that a number of people would follow him. He broke into a friend's house and stole his gun, a portable telephone and a tee shirt. He indicated that he then headed to Western Maryland, stopping to see some relatives in Cumberland, Maryland, had thoughts about breaking into a house and setting up a spiritual community and picked up a Caucasian hitchhiker thinking that this was a "black-white confrontation" and felt that the results of this encounter would determine "how things would turn out between blacks and whites in the world." He stated that he drove as far as Detroit, got gas but did not pay for it, "I felt someone in the gas station was paying it for me" and felt that the fact that no one followed him when he left the gas station was confirmation of the fact that somebody recognized his spiritual importance and was paying for his gasoline. He indicated that he returned to

To: Frank Howard, Esquire
         States Attorney of Howard County
Re: Richard Johnson

Baltimore on July 1, 1995 and noted that his father's car was parked near the family home. He stated that he was "spiritually off Baltimore time," drove around the city in order to "go in a different direction spiritually," felt that different cars had different spiritual messages and eventually went to see Donna. He then stated that he went home to see his parents. He stated that the following morning, he realized that his own family was a spiritual family and that he had to leave home in order to "find my own chemistry." He stated that he felt the music industry was going on a beach tour and that he needed a different car, specifically a BMW, because the BMW stood for black men working. He stated that his friend, Robert, who owned a BMW and lived in Columbia, Maryland, would give him this BMW. He noted that he drove down to Columbia with these thoughts in mind, parked a block away from Robert's home and "tried to kick the door down. I wanted to get the keys and leave quickly." He stated that his close friend, Harold, was there and that he did not expect him to be there. He stated that he told them to "give me the keys to the car," as he was holding the gun, and then he "heard the gun go off." He stated that he rushed out of the house, subsequently ran back into the house, pulling the telephone out of the wall, thinking that the police would have heard the gunshot. He stated that he then went to a hotel on Route One in Laurel because "this hour needed to pass," noting that the next hour would be better for him. He figured that everyone in the past was in the past hour. He stated that he saw the police but "I did not know why they were there." He stated that following his arrest, when he was interviewed by Detective Lois Palmer, she said that he had been arrested for the shooting of his friend and he responded, "The shooting of what friend?"

        In summary, then, while there is clear evidence of an extensive delusional system, and very bizarre thinking and behavior, verified not only by Mr. Johnson's recollections but also by other people's accounts, as well as by his own diaries contemporaneous with this period of time, there does not appear to be any clear linkage of the delusional thinking to the offense. Clearly, his taking Robert's car, the BMW, is tied to his delusion about needing such a car to go on a spiritual journey because BMW stood for "black men working," but there does not appear to be any substantial relationship of any of the delusional thinking to the actual thoughts about the victim, Mr. Harold Barnes. In fact, I returned to this theme on several occasions with Mr. Johnson and until the very last interview he insisted that the shooting of Harold was accidental. He specifically stated, for instance, that the delusional thinking "did not apply to Harold, it applied to everyone." He described the fact that everything had

Page 5
July 30, 1996

To: Frank Howard, Esquire
         States Attorney of Howard County
Re: Richard Johnson

changed and, in fact, stated that he did not know that Harold was even at Robert's home. He stated that everything had changed in his life and that "a love lifestyle" had been given to him. He denied being jealous of Harold, which he noted was the prosecution's theory of the case.

I confronted Mr. Johnson with the fact that he had mentioned to a former psychiatrist who had examined him for the Medical Office that there were apparently some homosexual thoughts regarding Harold. He acknowledged that such thoughts had occurred but that they had been approximately three months prior to the shooting. He insisted that these thoughts had never recurred, that he rarely, if ever, had thoughts about homosexuality and they most certainly were not occurring at the time of the offense. When asked about Harold's statement, "I love you," at the time of the shooting, Mr. Johnson in fact, stated that he did not experience this as a homosexual statement but rather that he was "putting my name out there to be challenged," which he described as "the more he said my name, the more I would be tested."

Notably, it was not until my most recent interview with Mr. Johnson, in May of 1996, that he made any connection whatsoever between the shooting and his delusional system. This occurred only after I had on two different occasions indicated to him that while I saw him as having serious mental abnormalities, I could not see the connection between these abnormalities and the shooting. In short, his "tying in" of the shooting to his delusional thinking appeared to occur only after prodding from me, rather than its having happened spontaneously. On this occasion, he again described the extensive delusional thinking on his drive down to Columbia, the BMW delusion and, in fact, even expanded it to the fact that he was driving behind a Honda Odyssey and that he felt that part of the crew of his spiritual journey were stars and were riding in that van. He felt that Robert's car was "there for anyone who wanted to get into the game." He felt that he was no longer Richard Johnson but was somebody whom he called "Johnny B." He indicated that he had to go into the house, wave the gun, get the keys and go, and when asked why he needed the gun, he stated, "They had a finesse game, but I had a power game." He stated that he parked a block away because, "I didn't want them to know about my car," and stated that he kicked in the door and was going to take the keys to Robert's car. He stated that when Harold asked him what was going on, "I got perturbed. This was putting out a challenge to me, to any spiritual opportunity I had." He stated that Harold saying his name got in the way of his spiritual journey. He stated that he still did not remember the second shot.

Page 6
July 30, 1996

To: Frank Howard, Esquire
         States Attorney of Howard County
Re: Richard Johnson

Mr. Johnson described prior arrests as having involved possession of marijuana on two occasions and driving on a suspended license on one occasion.

He denied any prior psychiatric history but indicated that his brother had been diagnosed as Paranoid Schizophrenia and had been treated at Sheppard Pratt, at University of Maryland Hospital and at Gundry Hospital, all in Baltimore, and at some hospital in New York which Mr. Johnson could not recall. He indicated that his brother had been taking both pills and injections of medication. He described his brother as easily agitated, impatient, shaking, dressing poorly, being paranoid and responding to voices.

Regarding his own drug involvement, Mr. Johnson described himself as a regular social user of marijuana, stating that it helped him relax the agitation caused by his mental illness. He noted that he had used cocaine between 1986 and 1988, moving from powder to freebasing, but stated that that was a bad experience and gave him "bad shakes." He denied any subsequent usage of cocaine, though, as will later be noted, several friends indicate that there was more recent cocaine usage.

Mr. Johnson denied any history of head trauma and any periods of loss of consciousness or exposure to toxic chemicals. He denied a wide variety of symptoms suggestive of neurological dysfunction but did notice frequent experiences of depersonalization while he was actively psychotic.

Mr. Johnson was born on June 24, 1966 in New York City, the youngest of four siblings. He stated that, as noted above, his parents had separated and, in fact, his father had remarried. His father's second wife had two sons and Mr. Johnson stated that he regarded them as brothers. His parents were separated in approximately 1977 and remarried in 1992. Mr. Johnson denied recalling much of his childhood but stated that his mother was a schoolteacher and his father a director of the organization N.A.A.C.P. He stated that the family came to Maryland when he was two years of age, at which time his father was the director of Maryland Public Radio and subsequently left to run for public office. Mr. Johnson seems to have very little knowledge about these early years, stating that he does not know much about the separation, "maybe he was cheating, but I don't know for sure." He stated that he had a good relationship with his parents, that he respected them and cared about them and even after the separation would see his father on a regular basis. He denied having any serious illnesses or injuries as a child. He stated that he lived in southwest

To: Frank Howard, Esquire
         States Attorney of Howard County
Re: Richard Johnson

Baltimore and went to school in that area. He stated that his grades were good in elementary school, that in middle school they fell off due to his friends and "procrastination," but noted that he had average grades in high school. He stated that he had many friends and socialized with everyone in his class. He noted that enuresis was a problem until the ninth grade and that he was shy, not having many girlfriends. He stated that his first girlfriend was in his senior year of high school. Again, as noted above, he had no memory of his reaction to his parents' separation, stating, "Maybe that's why my grades dropped." He graduated from high school in 1984 and entered Morgan State University in what at that time was a new engineering program. He stated that he dropped out of school for a year, working as a teller at Loyola Federal, obtained a student loan, returned to school and graduated in 1991. He stated that he worked for First Mariner Bank, began teaching and started attending University of Maryland in order to obtain a Master's Degree in Special Education.

Interviews With Collateral Sources:

          Ms. Wilma Shelton, Chief Psychologist at the Howard County Detention Center, described Mr. Johnson at the time of his admission as depressed but not showing evidence of psychotic thinking or behavior. She described him as appropriate, coherent, college educated and articulate.

          Mrs. Helen Johnson, the defendant's mother, was interviewed on February 23, 1996, and noted bizarre behavior on her son's part as far back as the Fall of 1993, recalling that he would get agitated, stating that he could read negative thoughts of others. She noted that he would frequently talk about hearing voices and that her husband, Mr. Johnson's father, obtained a list of "black Christian psychiatrists" but apparently Mr. Johnson never followed through with an appointment. She described her son as acting quite strangely, that he would take off and drive places, that he continued to hallucinate, but that his behavior was quite different from her son, Stephen, who had been diagnosed as Paranoid Schizophrenia. She stated that Stephen would pace, get agitated, have difficulty sleeping, behaviors that were quite distinct from Richard's behavior, which she described as withdrawn. She was concerned that he might be using drugs and noted that one week before the shooting she had had a confrontation with him about his not looking for a job. She stated that she had given him three months to find a job or he had to move out of the home. She stated that he became very angry with her at that point. She spoke about his describing a "dark cloud" coming over him the week

To: Frank Howard, Esquire
        States Attorney of Howard County
Re: Richard Johnson

before the shooting. She described the several days just prior to the shooting when Mr. Johnson had left town and driven to Detroit. She stated that her cousin, who lived in Cumberland, Maryland, described Mr. Johnson as "seeming to be high on drugs and very confused." She indicated that when he returned on Saturday, June 30th, she was very concerned about his bizarre behavior and that he agreed to see a psychiatrist Monday morning. She stated that she told him to get dressed, which he did, and stated that he walked out of the house, down an alley and disappeared. This was just prior to his drive to Columbia and the shooting.

I interviewed Mr. Johnson's father, Mr. Walter Johnson, on February 23, 1996. He stated that he has only recently noticed his son's illness, when his son told the parents that he was Jesus Christ. He stated, "We tried to get him help, but he refused." He described his son as hearing things from the television and radio, and becoming moody, quiet and depressed. He described his son as becoming progressively more paranoid, "spaced out and looking high." He stated that he insisted that his son admit himself to the hospital. He noted that when he would talk about being Jesus Christ, he was coherent, aware of what he was saying and was not argumentative. He, like his wife, said that Richard's behavior was quite different from Stephen's behavior. He stated that Richard's bizarre behavior evolved gradually, while Stephen's was very abrupt and acute. He stated that his son, Richard, was convinced that he was Jesus Christ. He denied that his son used drugs, with the exception of occasionally smoking pot. He denied any indication that his son was ever violent.

Officer Robert Stanton, the arresting officer, did note that at the time of arrest Mr. Johnson's face was "blank" and that his affect appeared flat. He stated that at the same time Mr. Johnson would not look at anyone, nor would he say anything. He indicated that Mr. Johnson did not look to him like the sort of actively psychotic individual who would need to be transported to Spring Grove Hospital.

I interviewed Mr. Stephen Johnson, Richard's older brother, on February 23, 1996. He indicated that he had had a serious problem with mental illness for the past fifteen years and that he would talk to his brother, Richard, about the things that he was going through. He indicated that he could also "see the illness in Richard." He again described Richard as "shutting down" rather than becoming violent or agitated. He stated that his brother, Richard, would say that he was the immaculate conception and that when Stephen would tell him that that was impossible, Richard would become angry but he never felt the anger would turn

Page 9
July 30, 1996

To: Frank Howard, Esquire
        States Attorney of Howard County
Re: Richard Johnson

into violence. In fact, Stephen indicated that on one occasion he tried to provoke Richard into a fight but Richard would just cry. He denied having any knowledge of Richard using cocaine and stated that when his brother would smoke marijuana, he would become "irritable and fussy but not violent."

I interviewed Detective Lois Palmer on March 8, 1996. At the time of interrogation, she stated that Mr. Johnson was quiet, put his head down, wept a bit and was trembling but she did not see anything unusual in his behavior. She indicated that he did not appear to her to be high on drugs and that she did not see any bizarre speech or behavior in his self-presentation.

I interviewed George Johnson, Richard's older brother, on March 8, 1996. He stated that "everyone in the family knows about Richard's mental illness" and that he, George, found out about the severity of his problems in February of 1995 when he stated that he became aware of Richard hearing things, hearing voices coming out of automobile tires and telling the pastor that he was Jesus Christ. He stated that his brother, Richard, would promise to get help but never did. Again, he stated that Richard would experiment with marijuana but he did not know about other drug usage. He stated that, again, Richard's behavior was much different from Stephen's behavior because the acting-out behavior which was quite typical of Stephen was atypical for Richard, even when he was hallucinating.

I interviewed Mr. Johnson's cousin, David Williams, on March 8, 1996. Mr. Williams described Richard as "weird," that he would "say things that were off the wall." He described periodic use of marijuana on Richard's part and stated that Richard would "fade in and out." He stated that during the week when Richard drove to Detroit, he, Mr. Williams, received bizarre telephone calls from Richard and that he would frequently seem nonresponsive and "in his own little world."

On March 8, 1996, I also interviewed John and Cathy Sanders, cousins of Mr. Johnson who lived in Cumberland, Maryland. They noted that on June 30, 1995, at four o'clock in the morning, he showed up and they were struck by the fact that he had shaved his head and lost weight. They described him as confused, saying one thing, retracting it, then saying something else. They described him as nervous and fidgety, unable to sit still, talking about his future, abruptly jumping from one topic to another, looking restless, haggard, "wired" and cagey. Mr. Sanders wondered whether or not Richard was on drugs because he stated that

To: Frank Howard, Esquire
         States Attorney of Howard County
Re: Richard Johnson

Mr. Johnson was scratching and could not sit still. He recalled that at his grandfather's funeral, Mr. Johnson had been talking loudly and inappropriately.

I interviewed Mary Carson, one of Mr. Johnson's girlfriends, on March 8, 1996. She stated that they had met in April of 1994, that she had moved into his home in February of 1995 and that their relationship had dissolved in April of 1995. She stated that while he was initially confident and well-groomed, his behavior got "weird" and his appearance deteriorated. She found out that he had quit his job in January of 1995. She stated that they would have conversations which he later would not be able to recall. She described him as talking to himself, mumbling and accusing her of having relationships which she did not have. He talked about a variety of strange ideas, his being isolated, in his own world, and, while she became aware of his unusual and bizarre journals and diaries, stating that Mr. Johnson never shared his religious ideas with her. She indicated that he would smoke marijuana two to three times a week, that she did not notice any particular impact drugs had on him and that she did not have any knowledge of his using any other drugs. She stated that he was very close to the decedent, Harold, and that there was no evidence of jealousy on Mr. Johnson's part. She noted that the entire family was in denial about the history of mental illness in the family and that the mother would minimize Mr. Johnson's periods of silence or periods when he would "go off." She noted that the most striking feature was Mr. Johnson withdrawing from everyone and from everything.

On the same date, I interviewed Ms. Fara Colton, Mr. Johnson's older sister. She noted that she became aware of his bizarre ideas in 1994 and in 1995 she became aware of his auditory hallucinations. She described him as having racing thoughts, agitation and again, consistent with others, the fact that while Mr. Johnson would talk fast and have racing thoughts, he would not act-out based on his mental illness. She also noted a family history of mental illness, including a maternal grandfather, a maternal aunt, several maternal cousins and on the father's side, an uncle, three cousins and two great uncles.

On March 14, 1996, I interviewed Donna Nast, Mr. Johnson's most recent girlfriend. She indicated that she had met Mr. Johnson on May 1, 1995 at the wedding of a mutual friend. She described him as "cute and shy" and, on their very first date, "I saw something wrong, he was loose and scattered, nothing made sense." He described himself to her as "the King," talked about the cosmic essence of being and this behavior would persist. For instance, she described what appeared to be

Page 11
July 30, 1996

To: Frank Howard, Esquire
          States Attorney of Howard County
Re: Richard Johnson

auditory hallucinations, "It looked like he was responding to things and laughing inappropriately." She described him as not showing any jealousy toward Harold, in fact, showing high admiration for him. She indicated that he was quite upset about his mother having put him out of the house and described his leaving town with her rental car. She indicated that when he did not return, she spoke with Mr. Johnson's mother, who told her at that time about his hearing messages from the television set. Ms. Nast indicated that Mr. Johnson needed to be evaluated but "she refused and would not call the police." Ms. Nast described the fact that when Mr. Johnson came to her apartment on Saturday, the day before the shooting, he looked wild, appeared to be hallucinating, admitted to racing thoughts, had a sing-song quality in the way he responded to her questions and admitted that he needed to go into the hospital. She indicated that she did not have any further contact until she was called by Detective Lois Palmer, who asked whether Mr. Johnson had a mental illness. She described Mr. Johnson as frequently smoking marijuana but did not describe usage of any other drugs. She indicated specifically that she could not imagine why Richard would kill anyone and that especially he never had any delusional thoughts about Harold. She stated that she had seen in his notebooks his "imploring God to stop the voices." She described Mr. Johnson as sweet, gentle and passive, and that violence was totally unlike him.

On March 15, 1996, I interviewed Ms. Lily Thompson. She described Mr. Johnson as being "weird" and that she had only dated him for three months in 1993. She indicated that he had talked to her about hearing voices, that he was paranoid, that he always thought people were talking about him or looking at him. She stated that at times he would seem comfortable with the voices and at other times they would bother him, that he seemed distressed and "he was too weird for me." She described him as at times dressing well and at other times being disheveled, but that she never saw any evidence of violent tendencies. She stated that he was best friends with Harold, that they were like brothers and cared a lot for each other. She stated that she had never seen him with any drugs and she was unaware of his problems at work.

On April 25, 1996, I interviewed Ms. Sandra Towns, who was present at the shooting, and she described Mr. Johnson as "goofy, quirky, hokey and silly" but not showing evidence of mental illness. She stated that he had low self-esteem, that Mr. Johnson admired Harold Barnes and that while Mr. Johnson would sometimes appear disheveled, she never saw him as unusual. She described him as smoking marijuana and drinking beer and as being unreliable, though he was intelligent. At the time of

To: Frank Howard, Esquire
         States Attorney of Howard County
Re: Richard Johnson

the shooting, she described Richard as breaking down the door and that he "looked calculating, like he was on a mission." She described him as angry and felt that the motive for the shooting was jealousy. She stated that while she had no personal knowledge of drug usage, she had heard about Mr. Johnson's drug usage.

Finally, I consulted with Doctor Peter Raines regarding his inter-view of Robert Rogers. He also did not see Mr. Johnson as mentally ill, rather feeling that Mr. Johnson was jealous about Harold and "he knew what he was doing." He also did not know about Mr. Johnson's drug usage. He stated that he was convinced that Mr. Johnson knew what he was doing.

Grand Jury Testimony:

1. Testimony of Robert Morris

Robert Morris was a friend of Mr. Johnson, who had met him at the University of Maryland. He described Mr. Johnson's crime as being "out of character," stating that he "was nice, having no malice or ill will to anyone." He described Mr. Johnson as mumbling some-thing to himself and getting totally off the subject when one would try to have a conversation with him. He denied knowledge of any drug problems, although he stated that Mr. Johnson would occa-sionally smoke marijuana.

2. Testimony of Bart Davis

Mr. Davis is a colleague of Mr. Johnson, the principal of Anton High School. He stated that Mr. Johnson had difficulty taking direc-tion from the staff, but had good relationships with the students. He described unusual behavior, disorientation, deterioration and "dreaminess." Mr. Davis thought that Richard Johnson was on drugs but had no independent verification of that.

3. Testimony of William Carter

Doctor Carter is a university professor at the University of Mary-land, who indicated that on one occasion following the termination of a contract that Mr. Johnson had at Maryland, Mr. Johnson ap-peared at Doctor Carter's home, his pupils dilated, looking "wired"

Page 13
July 30, 1996

To: Frank Howard, Esquire
        States Attorney of Howard County
Re: Richard Johnson

as if he were on drugs. Doctor Carter described Mr. Johnson as being "very much into the Bible."

4. Testimony of Ann Shaw

Ann Shaw is the Head of the Mathematics Department at Anton High School. She described Mr. Johnson as showing erratic behavior, coming in late for work, sometimes not showing up at all and not calling in. She described him as usually quiet but getting very upset, aggressive and out of control when he was instructed not to use a computer at the school. She indicated that he had spoken about personal problems on which he would not elaborate and that on one occasion he left for two days and no one was able to locate him. She stated that she thought that he was on drugs, that he would doze off in faculty meetings and "looked spacey all the time."

5. Testimony of Gary James

Mr. James is a business manager and coach at Anton High School. He also thought that Mr. Johnson was on drugs because he would fall asleep in class, would leave class and on one occasion asked him where he could obtain some drugs, specifically cocaine. He indicated that one week before the offense, he saw Mr. Johnson in a heavy drug area in Baltimore and that Mr. Johnson looked high, dirty and unshaven.

6. Testimony of Donna Nast

As noted above, Donna Nast was Mr. Johnson's most recent girlfriend prior to his arrest. Ms. Nast described Mr. Johnson as frequently being unclear, his thoughts not connecting with one another and his being quite bizarre. She described him as having a close friendship with Harold and again described Mr. Johnson as scattered, admitting to racing thoughts, nonresponsive and as demonstrating in his writings grandiosity, ideas of reference and feelings of omnipotence.

7. Testimony of Randall Norton

Mr. Norton was a friend of Mr. Johnson from school. He noted that someone had told him in November of 1994 that Mr. Johnson was heavily into cocaine and that in May of 1995 Mr. Johnson looked

To: Frank Howard, Esquire
         States Attorney of Howard County
Re: Richard Johnson

"out of it." He described Mr. Johnson's preoccupations with radio and TV signals which were trying to get people to do certain things and that Mr. Johnson felt that the television signals were talking to him. He talked about the voices with Mr. Norton but Mr. Norton felt that his condition was "different from the spaced-out feeling that is associated with drugs."

8.   Testimony of Robert Sutton

Mr. Sutton was a friend of both Mr. Johnson and Harold Barnes at University of Maryland. He described Mr. Johnson as demonstrating problematic behavior in approximately 1993, that his attitude started changing and he became irritable. He described Mr. Johnson as having rambling talk, looking weird and buying large quantities of cocaine.

9.   Testimony of Mary Carson

As noted earlier, Mary Carson was Mr. Johnson's girlfriend between April 1994 and March 1995. She described his starting to withdraw in December of 1994 and demonstrating erratic behavior in 1995. She stated he would talk to himself, write strange rambling things and would gesture, smile and frown. She described him as increasingly paranoid and was convinced that this was not the effects of drugs.

10. Testimony of Karl Retton

Mr. Retton was a close friend of Mr. Johnson, who met him at University of Maryland and he described cocaine usage on Mr. Johnson's part four or five times between 1991 and 1995 and specifically recalled cocaine usage in December of 1994. He also noted that in the Summer of 1993, he became aware of the fact that Mr. Johnson was experiencing auditory hallucinations.

11. Testimony of Harold Aston

Mr. Aston was a classmate of Mr. Johnson both in high school and in college, and was his roommate for a while in his parents' home. He also described Mr. Johnson as acting strangely and that he, Mr. Aston, did not feel that it was the result of drugs. He would make strange comments, such as "starting the rapture," would lock

To: Frank Howard, Esquire
          States Attorney of Howard County
Re: Richard Johnson

himself in his room and ask Mr. Aston whether or not he believed in evil spirits. He believed that the devil was talking through a television, would hear voices and talked about the signals that he was receiving. Mr. Aston said that Mr. Johnson would also laugh and mumble to himself, like he was "not really part of the conversation."

Psychological Testing:

On the Wechsler Adult Intelligence Scale, Revised Form, Mr. Johnson obtains a verbal IQ of 96, a performance IQ of 105 and a resultant full-scale IQ of 99, placing him within the average range of intellectual functioning. There is exceedingly wide variation in his subtest scaled scores, suggesting variable attention and concentration, as well as peculiarity in reasoning. All of the neuropsychological screening tests are essentially within normal limits, though there are some results suggestive of impairments of attention and concentration, but in light of the rest of the negative findings, this is most likely a function of the underlying mental illness rather than any organic problems. Projective testing reveals an individual with no current overt signs of psychosis, who presents a valid, though somewhat depressed record. He prefers delay, reflection, control, ideational and fantasy approaches, rather than acting-out. Stress tolerance is adequate and it appears that he is currently extremely affectively withdrawn. There is evidence of underlying cognitive impairment and his ability to analyze the stimulus field and organize the world around him efficiently are currently intact. There is no current evidence of thought disorder on the testing, though he does tend to show somewhat of a defensive flight into fantasy, a tendency to intellectualize affective experience, withdraw into himself and had difficulty engaging in cooperative interactions. Significant depressive symptoms are also present. He demonstrates very poor judgment, a tendency toward rather vague thought processes and some evidence of paranoia in his abstract thinking.

The Minnesota Multiphasic Personality Inventory reveals a valid profile consistent with an individual who is somewhat hysterical and histrionic, testing as strongly repressed and overcontrolled. There is evidence at times of a dissociative lack of self-awareness in that he may be unaware of what he is doing and the consequences of his actions. Expressions of anger would be rationalized, if not self-righteous, with a denial of hostile intentions. This test pattern has been associated at times with paranoid trends and brief paranoid episodes that include projections, suspicions and excessive jealousies but little, if any, breakdown of reality testing or disorganization of behavior. Currently, many of the defenses

To: Frank Howard, Esquire
          States Attorney of Howard County
Re: Richard Johnson

against the underlying psychosis are expressed through somatization. The profile, as noted above, suggests hysterical and dissociative trends and emotionally explosive episodes, but in some cases similar profiles have been obtained in controlled and covered-over phases following acute emotional upheavals. In other words, this profile is consistent with someone who is in an unstable remission from an acute paranoid episode.

The Structured Interview of Reported Symptoms is also consistent, presenting a profile of honest responding, no evidence of malingering and, in fact, a tendency to minimize even everyday problems.

In summary, then, there are ample indications that Mr. Johnson has a severe underlying mental illness from which he is currently in a state of rather unstable remission. Furthermore, from the descriptions of not only Mr. Johnson but a wide variety of collateral sources, he was demonstrating symptoms of this psychotic disorder around the time of the alleged offenses. It would be fair to say that he was actively psychotic during that period of time. In fact, one of the offenses, namely stealing Robert Rogers' car, was clearly tied to his delusional thinking about the BMW standing for black men working and, in reference to this offense, Mr. Johnson clearly lacked substantial capacity to appreciate the wrongfulness of his behavior or to conform his behavior to the requirements of the law.

However, in reference to the shooting of Harold Barnes, there does not appear to be such a clear linkage between the psychosis and the crime. In fact, Mr. Johnson repeatedly denied over the course of at least three interviews any connection between his delusional thinking, his hallucinations and the shooting of Harold. He maintained steadfastly that it was an accident. It was only after the present examiner indicated his questions about the fact that such a link did not exist that Mr. Johnson appears to have "manufactured" such a link. Therefore, in reference to the shooting of Harold Barnes, while he was actively psychotic, it is my opinion that he possessed the capacity to appreciate the wrongfulness of his behavior and conform his behavior to the requirements of the law. There is no evidence, in my opinion, that the shooting of Mr. Barnes was in any way a product of his active mental illness.

Page 17
July 30, 1996

To: Frank Howard, Esquire
        States Attorney of Howard County
Re: Richard Johnson

I trust the above analysis is of some assistance to you. Please feel free to call on me if you need further information.

Very truly yours,

David L. Shapiro, PhD
Diplomate in Forensic Psychology
American Board of Professional
Psychology

DLS:esp

c.c.:   Peter Raines, MD

DAVID L. SHAPIRO, PhD
DIPLOMATE IN FORENSIC PSYCHOLOGY
AMERICAN BOARD OF PROFESSIONAL PSYCHOLOGY
1498-M REISTERTOWN ROAD
MAIL BOX 274
BALTIMORE, MARYLAND 21208

Telephone: (410) 653-5673

April 20, 1997

David Samuels, Esquire
Public Defender Service
451 Indiana Avenue, N.W.
Washington, DC 20001-2775

Re: Harry Martin

Dear Mr. Samuels:

Pursuant to your referral, I have completed my psychological evaluation of your client, Mr. Harry Martin, whom I examined at the Forensic Center on three occasions: February 16, 1997; March 16, 1997 and March 20, 1997. In addition to clinical interview and history-taking, I administered the following psychological tests: Minnesota Multiphasic Personality Inventory; Luria-Nebraska Neuropsychological Battery; Wechsler Adult Intelligence Scale, Revised Form; the Rorschach and the Projective Drawings.

In addition, I reviewed the records at the Forensic Center, as well as the records from the Georgetown University Hospital, which you had provided me, and I also reviewed the psychiatric records from Mr. Martin's earlier hospitalizations while he still lived in New York. I also interviewed by telephone Mr. David Clinton, Mr. Martin's uncle, the individual who perhaps knew Mr. Martin best and had been with him in the days immediately preceding the offense.

As you know, Mr. Martin is charged with the homicide of his landlady, in early January of 1997. Shortly thereafter, Mr. Martin admitted himself to the psychiatric unit of the Georgetown University Hospital, telling the staff that he had a dream about the death of his landlady. There was apparently evidence of exceedingly bizarre behavior on Mr. Martin's part in the days immediately preceding the homicide. A woman named Karen Myers, who also lived in the same building as Mr. Martin, indicated that Mr. Martin on the night before the offense was throwing things around the kitchen and then stated that he wanted to talk to her. When she refused to talk to him, he grabbed her wrist and started punching her in the chest, as well as hitting her in the head. Ms. Myers indicated that Mr. Martin had threatened to hurt her the very first day that she moved into the house, stating that he was the manager of the house

To: David Samuels, Esquire
        Public Defender Service
Re: Harry Martin

and that Karen had better keep the kitchen clean, "or I will hurt you." Apparently, another roommate had to restrain Mr. Martin so that he would not hit Karen. He continued to threaten her, and she needed the police on several occasions. She indicated that Mr. Martin would be erratic at one moment and then normal the next, and that by the time the police arrived he would always appear intact. She stated that he used to pace around the house, talking to himself, laughing and then would scream in an irrational manner at people. She also recalled that on the day before the offense, Mr. Martin was calling many girls and asking them out for that evening, but apparently was not able to find a woman to go out with him.

During the several occasions when I examined and tested Mr. Martin, he was consistently pleasant, cooperative and well-oriented. He indicated that he was feeling better due to the medication and treatment, and indicated that he is taking Lithium Carbonate, Haldol and Thorazine. He was informed of the nonconfidential nature of the interview, that I would be preparing a report for his attorney and he consented to the examination.

Mr. Martin noted that his first hospitalization occurred when he was twenty years of age in New York, with his becoming depressed and suicidal, as well as experiencing auditory hallucinations and paranoid ideation. He stated, "I felt like everybody was looking at me and thinking about doing something dangerous to me." He stated that he could not recall what the voices told him, but he recalls becoming violent on occasions and having to enter the hospital. He indicated that on one occasion, when his father visited him in the hospital and woke him up, he jumped out of bed and beat him. He was in the hospital for several weeks and recalled having ideas about God and about prophets. He thought that he was either God or a prophet or a messenger of God. He signed himself out, took medication for a few months, then stopped the medication and felt that he was all right. He stated that shortly thereafter he came to Washington, and he described developing problems in which he stated, "I was a listener, I couldn't talk, I would get confused and dizzy and violent, and people talked to me too much." He stated that it all crashed in on him and that he could not understand what was being said. He spoke of his inability to look at people's eyes because "it made me dizzy."

When Mr. Martin came to Washington, he said there was a period of time when he felt happy living with his uncle, Mr. Clinton, and working as an auto mechanic, going to school as an undergraduate. He stated, however, that his grades started slipping, that he could not concentrate, that he got confused and dizzy and that "the situation was just

To: David Samuels, Esquire
       Public Defender Service
Re: Harry Martin

like before," paranoid feelings, "people looking at me, thinking about hurting me and criticized me." He stated that this feeling got "wider and bigger, and then I felt like I was God and everybody else was either a bad guy or a good guy." He also thought that when people die, "the good people go to the moon and the bad people go to the sun." He added quite spontaneously, "That's how I killed my landlady, she was an evil person, I was God, I had to kill her and make her go to the sun." Mr. Martin indicated that he was under increasing stress in the months immediately preceding the offense, having gotten fired from a job and experiencing the return of his psychotic symptoms. He also stated that he had a girlfriend at the same time who had left him, telling him that he was not attentive to her because "you don't look at my eyes." He also recounted two previous hospitalizations at the Georgetown University Hospital in the months preceding the offense. Mr. Martin stated that his doctor at Georgetown had recommended that he be followed at the outpatient clinic, which he refused, but he eventually went to see a private psychiatrist and stopped taking the Lithium.

Mr. Martin described the offense itself in the following way. He stated that at first he was getting along well with his landlady, and then stated the he had an argument with Ms. Myers which he described as quite stressful, especially when the police arrived. He was able to obtain a job as an auto mechanic, worked for three months, but was then fired, stating that the stress he was under caused poor concentration and consequently his inability to handle his job. Mr. Martin described many paranoid feelings and that his landlady would continually do things, such as knocking on his door at 5:00 a.m., which added to his stress. He stated that after he was fired from his job, "the God thing started again." He stated that he had thoughts about Judgment Day, about the world coming to an end and about the fact that anyone around him could put him under stress. He described the feeling noted earlier that he was continually confused when other people would talk. He was continually talking about God, "People thought I was crazy," and he lost another job as a result of this, with his employer "thinking I was on drugs."

Mr. Martin recalls having an argument with his landlady, with her holding his keys, telling him to get out and calling the police. He stated that he was fighting to get the keys from her and that she had fallen down some stairs. He said that he vaguely recalls strangling her because "I wanted her to go to the sun and felt she was evil." He described her as a drug addict because she took prescription drugs and that she was greedy because "she wanted me to do things for her."

To: David Samuels, Esquire
         Public Defender Service
Re: Harry Martin

Mr. Martin described himself as a beast, an animal, who didn't care about anything. He stated that he thought of his landlady as the devil and that he was "like James Bond," that the whole world depended on him to carry out his mission. He stated that he had put his landlady's body onto a shelf and then got a phone call from a girl who wanted to come over and visit him, and recalls thinking that she, too, was the devil. He stated that he wanted to kill her, too, and that she backed off when he broke a bottle and threatened her.

He described the fact that "something was pushing me." He described this as an uncontrollable state in which he can't decide whether to do something or not do something, and that the only way that he can find comfort is to "finish the act." Mr. Martin did not describe the period of time during the offense as a blackout but rather as "a blur," and when he admitted himself to the Georgetown University Hospital he stated that he did not tell them about the crime because "I didn't think it was a crime, I was God and I was sending an evil person to the sun." He stated that he recalls telling the doctors that he had AIDS, which was a disease of the will and that he felt that he had this because "my will had been broken." Following his being in the Georgetown University Hospital one day, he stated that the police came and picked him up and took him to jail where, after one day, he was transferred to the Forensic Center.

Mr. Martin also described a number of very bizarre thoughts about his uncle at the time, thinking that his uncle was evil, and pulling a knife on his uncle. He stated that he thought that a beautiful girl would be at his uncle's home because he had killed all the devils. When he did not find a beautiful woman at his uncle's home, he stated that he pulled a knife, thinking that his uncle had done something to the girl.

Mental status examination revealed a neatly dressed, cooperative, well-oriented individual whose Attention, Perception and Memory were intact. His affect was notably blunted, but his speech was generally coherent. He seemed to be quite confused in terms of his time sequence. He reported a past history of auditory hallucinations, as well as paranoid ideation, and stated that he still has difficulty looking directly in people's eyes and gets confused when he tries to listen to other people talk to him. He did mention some olfactory hallucinations, "either a nice smell or a smell like tuna fish." He denied gustatory, tactile or visual hallucinations, and stated that he has had recent suicidal ideation, but has only made one suicide attempt.

To: David Samuels, Esquire
         Public Defender Service
Re: Harry Martin

  Mr. Martin reports that at the age of six he suffered a head injury when he went through a glass window. He was also involved in an automobile accident in September, 1995, in which he was apparently hit from behind and sustained a head injury in the frontal area. He was unconscious for several minutes and was hospitalized at the Alexandria Hospital. He indicated that a neurological workup was performed at Georgetown University Hospital and at the Neurological Associates but stated that as far as he was told, the results of all procedures were negative. Those records are not available at the time of the present preparation of this report.

  Mr. Martin reported frequent headaches which he described as "a cycle, every two or three hours." He stated that they are accompanied by dizziness and that they tend to go away by themselves. He also stated that the dizziness and headaches are associated with the same "blurry feeling" which he experienced at the time of the offense. He stated that he has had these "cycles" of headache and dizziness all his life, but that they have become worse and more pronounced since the automobile accident in September, 1995. He denied having any blackouts and stated that he has had only one seizure in his life, apparently a reaction to the Haldol that he was placed on at Georgetown University Hospital. He stated also that people have told him "all my life" about times when he would stare off into space, move his foot, turn his head left and right and cough, with his being unaware of either the blank spells or motions. He indicated that only on one occasion in his life has he been amnestic for a period of violence, this being the incident when he attacked his father while in the psychiatric facility in New York. He stated that he only described this incident because his father had told him what happened, but that he, himself, had no memory of it. Mr. Martin also described significant periods of right-left disorientation, and stated that this has been going on "all my life." He described occasional loss of control in his hands, and states that he has frequent fugue states approximately once weekly, though he has never found himself going more than short distances during these fugues. He also described frequent déjà vu experiences and somewhat less frequent, but still relatively regular, jamais vu experiences approximately once a month.

  Mr. Martin was born in Los Angeles, California on March 17, 1960, the older of two siblings. He stated that his father at that time was a student at U.C.L.A. His parents are alive and together, living in New York and Mr. Martin grew up in New York having returned there shortly after his birth. His father is currently a Professor of Sociology at the New York University. He stated that his mother was a high school teacher,

Page 6
April 20, 1997

To: David Samuels, Esquire
        Public Defender Service
Re: Harry Martin

that he was very close to her and that she would "pamper me a lot." Much of the time that Mr. Martin was growing up his father was in school studying. He dated the onset of his psychological problems to the time when his father obtained his degree. Mr. Martin's brother is much younger than he, and Mr. Martin denies feeling any particular upset at the birth of his younger sibling.

Mr. Martin completed high school in New York and recalls having difficulty concentrating even then. He reflected that perhaps this was due to the head injury that he had sustained there. He described himself as a rather shy individual who kept pretty much to himself, had one or two close friends, no girlfriends and generally maintained about a C average in school.

As noted previously, Mr. Martin was first hospitalized in New York in 1980. He was described at that time as quite withdrawn, show-ing much deterioration in personal hygiene, and having the delusion that his face was ugly. He was treated with electroconvulsive therapy, Stelazine and Tofranil, and was urged to move to Washington to live with his uncle, and get away from his dominant father. He apparently eloped from the hospital, but returned several days later, was hospitalized for another month and was described as quite confused, with a final diagnosis of an Acute Schizophrenic Episode.

As noted earlier, there were two hospitalizations at the Georgetown University Hospital prior to the one which followed the of-fense. He was first hospitalized there in May of 1996, at which time he spoke of anxiety, the fact that his personality kept changing, that he had difficulty working, that he was losing friends and was going into violent rages. A neurological work-up revealed some rather inconsistent findings among the various diagnostic procedures, and the patient was described as having paranoid and somatic delusions, as well as thoughts of assault-ing others. During the course of hospitalization, he was described as agi-tated, delusional and having many "racing thoughts." He was diagnosed at that time as a Bipolar Affective Disorder, and was referred for outpa-tient treatment with a Doctor Brooks with whom Mr. Martin remained in treatment from June of 1996 apparently until fairly close to the time of the offense. When he was admitted on January 4, 1997, he complained about the fact that his heart was going to stop, that he was trying to find God, wanted to touch the sun and he was characterized as having loos-ened associations, flight of ideas, delusions and hallucinations. He spoke of a split between his body and soul; the troubling visions about his land-lady; his attacking his girlfriend with a bottle and the fact that his former

To: David Samuels, Esquire
        Public Defender Service
Re: Harry Martin

psychiatrist, Doctor Brooks, was evil because he gave him impure medication. Mr. Martin refused a psychological test because he said that if he took it, "principles will collide and that will put us above a higher power, and no one should put themselves above God." On the ward, he was described as loose, tangential, grandiose, delusional, and on one occasion he burst out of the seclusion room, knocked over a chair, ran to the nursing station, attempted to assault a staff member and would alternately assume a boxing and karate stance.

Following his arrest, imprisonment and transfer to the Forensic Center, he was described on January 7, 1997, in a Forensic Psychiatry Report, as being in a dream-like state in which he could not distinguish fantasy and reality, and reiterated the fact that both his former psychiatrist and his uncle were evil. His affect was described as flat and there was evidence of paranoid delusions, impaired reality testing and marked concerns about his ability to stand trial.

In a report dated February 26, 1997, following approximately seven weeks of treatment, Mr. Martin is described as competent to stand trial.

I interviewed Mr. Martin's uncle, Mr. David Clinton, by telephone, and he was of the opinion that Mr. Martin had not been "normal" for many years following the automobile accident. Mr. Clinton indicated that, at that time, his nephew became grandiose, confused reality and fantasy and started having mood swings and lost interest in his appearance, symptoms that Mr. Clinton had not noted prior to the accident. Mr. Clinton stated further that Mr. Martin would use very foul language in inappropriate situations, notably to Mr. Clinton's wife; would become very suspicious; would have bizarre and grandiose ideas, such as his having discovered the origin of the universe. Mr. Martin would shout and scream on the telephone, start talking about suicide and would occasionally be violent.

Mr. Clinton stated that on the same day that the homicide occurred, his nephew was experiencing hallucinations and had actually threatened Mr. Clinton's wife with a knife. Mr. Clinton states now, in retrospect, that he did not realize it was a delusion on his nephew's part when Mr. Martin had told him that he had become the manager of an apartment building and was collecting rent. Mr. Clinton said that following Mr. Martin's having attacked Ms. Myers he begged to stay in Mr. Clinton's home because he was afraid his landlady would call the police.

Page 8
April 20, 1997

To: David Samuels, Esquire
         Public Defender Service
Re: Harry Martin

Mr. Clinton confirmed the absence states and said that Mr. Martin would have them all the time, "spacing out, shifting his head constantly, shaking his leg and being unaware of it." He stated that on the day prior to the offense, Mr. Martin was breathing heavily and was totally unaware of this as well.

Mr. Clinton described his nephew's symptoms prior to the accident as "just having a lack of purpose," but following the accident, Mr. Clinton became afraid of him and concerned for his wife and for Mr. Martin's landlady. He described his nephew's difficulty concentrating, and stated that he often observed Mr. Martin pushing his head "to get rid of the voices." He described his nephew as wandering off and doing something else while he was trying to do a certain task, and said that his nephew would be quite forgetful in a variety of activities, such as trying to drive a car without putting the hood down.

While the Minnesota Multiphasic Personality Inventory initially appears to be invalid, in light of the other test data, and the neuropsychological data suggestive of Central Nervous System Impairment, this profile appears to be more a cry for help than any form of malingering. The SIRS scores were also in the "Honest" Range of Responding.

On the Wechsler Adult Intelligence Scale, Revised Form, Mr. Martin obtains a Verbal IQ of 82, a Performance IQ of 70 and a Resultant Full Scale IQ of 75, placing him within the Borderline range of intellectual functioning. This clearly appears to be severely depressed below Mr. Martin's actual capacity, with the depression occurring due to his mental illness and apparent brain impairment. There are many evidences of pathological intrusions, cognitive slippage, peculiar logic, confusion, impulsivity, tangential and irrelevant answers and many breakthroughs of rather primitive, destructive feeling.

Projective Drawings reveal an individual with a primitive, very poorly differentiated and distorted body image, and exceedingly poor reality testing despite extreme defensiveness and affective constriction and guardedness. That is, Mr. Martin makes a valiant attempt to ward off his underlying psychotic illness, but despite these massive efforts to control his illness, his reality testing and perceptual accuracy are greatly compromised. He tries to concentrate only on the precise details of a situation rather than attempting to organize it into any meaningful whole. When affective material is allowed into his perceptual world, it comes through in an unbound, primitive, destructive form. Despite, as noted above, all of

To: David Samuels, Esquire
         Public Defender Service
Re: Harry Martin

his attempts to defend against the underlying disorganization, there is still much evidence of autistic logic, neologistic thinking and precipitous losses of reality testing.

On the Luria-Nebraska Neuropsychological Battery, five of Mr. Martin's basic clinical scales are above the critical level, the Memory, Motor, Receptive Speech, Intellectual Processes and Visual scales. All of his summary scales also exceed the critical level, and the pattern of the summary scales suggests that he has made some partial recovery from his head trauma, but there are still major areas of dysfunction.

A localization analysis reveals diffuse impairment, with the impairment being more severe in the right hemisphere than in the left hemisphere. All of the right hemisphere scales exceed the critical level, with the left temporal area seeming to show some degree of impairment, followed by the left frontal area.

Specific areas of difficulty involve motor slowness; much evidence of spatial disorientation; difficulty coordinating instructions with various motor movements and a variety of difficulties in abstraction such as concept recognition, relating concepts to one another and being unable to understand what he reads. There is also evidence of severe memory problems across a variety of different tasks.

In summary, then, Mr. Harry Martin is a seriously disturbed individual, with evidence both of a major mental disorder, most likely a Schizo-affective Illness, coupled with strong suggestions of Central Nervous System Impairment. I would certainly recommend further neurological investigation as follow-up in this matter.

Based on the material available, however, the history of mental disorder and the extreme disorganization of behavior noted in the days immediately prior to the offense by Mr. Martin's uncle, it is my opinion that as a result of a mental disease (and possibly mental defect also), at the time of the offense Mr. Martin lacked substantial capacity to appreciate the wrongfulness of his behavior and to conform his behavior to the requirements of the law. The alleged offense, if committed by Mr. Martin, was in my opinion a product of his mental disease.

Page 10
April 20, 1997

To: David Samuels, Esquire
        Public Defender Service
Re: Harry Martin

     I trust the foregoing analysis is of some assistance to you. If I may be of further help, please do not hesitate to call on me.

                         Very truly yours,

                         David L. Shapiro, PhD
                         Diplomate in Forensic Psychology
                         American Board of Professional
                              Psychology

DLS:esp

c.c.:   Robert Nelson, MD
        Suite 206 - Padonia Centre
        30 East Padonia Road
        Timonium, MD 21093

APPENDIX F

<u>Test Publishers, Resources and Services</u>

TEST PUBLISHERS, RESOURCES AND SERVICES

The following tests and other resources are available from Psychological Assessment Resources, P.O. Box 998, Odessa, FL 33556-9901. Telephone: 800-331-8378. Fax: 800-727-9329. Web Site: www.parinc.com.

Exner, J. (1985). *Rorschach Structural Summary Blank.* Ashville, NC: Rorschach Workshops.

Exner, J. (1991) *The Rorschach, A Comprehensive System* (Vol. 2, 2nd ed.). New York: Wiley.

Exner, J. (1993) *The Rorschach, A Comprehensive System* (Vol. 1, 3rd ed.). New York: Wiley.

Exner, J. (1995a) *The Rorschach, A Comprehensive System* (Vol. 3, 2nd ed.). New York: Wiley.

Exner, J. (1995b). *Rorschach Interpretive Assistance Program (RIAP3 Plus) (Version 3.12).* Odessa, FL: Psychological Assessment Resources.

Exner, J. (1995c). *A Rorschach Workbook for the Comprehensive System* (4th ed.). Ashville, NC: Rorschach Workshops.

Green, R. (1988). *MMPI, Adult Interpretive System.* Odessa, FL: Psychological Assessment Resources.

Green, R. (1991). *MMPI-2/MMPI Interpretive Manual.* Old Tappan, NJ: Allyn & Bacon.

Green, R. (1998). *MMPI-2, Adult Interpretive System.* Odessa, FL: Psychological Assessment Resources.

Rogers, R. (1984). *Rogers Criminal Responsibility Assessment Scale.* Odessa, FL: Psychological Assessment Resources.

Rogers, R. (1992). *Structured Interview of Reported Symptoms.* Odessa, FL: Psychological Assessment Resources.

Other companies offering forensic-related materials include:

Multi-Health Systems, Inc., 908 Niagra Falls Boulevard, North Tonawanda, NY 14120-2060. Telephone: 800-456-3003. Fax: 888-540-4484 / 416-424-1736. Web Site: www.mhs.com.

NCS Assessments, P.O. Box 1416, Minneapolis, MN 55440. Telephone: 800-627-7271. Fax: 800-632-9011. Web Site: www.ncs.com.

The Psychological Corporation, 555 Academic Court, San Antonio, TX 78204-2498. Telephone: 800-211-8378. Fax: 800-232-1223. Web Site: www.psychcorp.com.

APPENDIX G

<u>Glossary</u>

GLOSSARY OF TERMS

Adjudicative Forum

A term used to describe what transpires in a court of law.

American Law Institute

A "think tank" that periodically proposes change in various laws. Its 1962 version of the insanity defense (Model Penal Code) was incorporated into the 1972 *Brawner* decision.

Attorney-Client Privilege

The privilege of confidentiality between attorney and client - anything a client says to her or his attorney is privileged unless there is an explicit waiver. When a psychologist or psychiatrist is retained by an attorney to perform an evaluation, all communications between that expert and the attorney are covered under the same "umbrella" of privilege unless waived.

Battered Spouse Syndrome

Term coined by Doctor Lenore Walker which described the psychological characteristics of a battered woman ("learned helplessness"), the reasons for her remaining in an abusive relationship and the three phases of the abusive relationship: increasing tension, acute battering and contrition/repentance, which tend to perpetuate the relationship.

Behavioral Science Profiling

A technique developed by the F.B.I. which involves developing hypotheses about classes of individuals who may have committed a particular crime, based on analysis of the crime scene. Data from the crime scene is analyzed in terms of other data gathered both from interview of violent offenders and demographic data characterizing such offenders.

Behavioral Sciences Unit - F.B.I.

The group responsible for the development of the preceding "profiling" techniques; originally called VICAP (Violent Crimes Apprehension Program).

Criminal Responsibility

Refers to state of mind at the time of the alleged offense - sometimes referred to as M.S.O. (mental state at time of the offense); the concept referred to under the rubric of the insanity defense.

Daubert vs. Merrell Dowe Pharmaceuticals

1993 case in which the Supreme Court of the United States ruled that the Frye test was "too austere" and held that the Federal Rules of Evidence should govern admissibility of expert testimony.

Diminished Capacity

A legal principle referring to the defendant's incapacity to form the "requisite specific intent" to commit a particular offense, that is the state of mind capable of deliberating and planning a specific crime. Some crimes, by definition, do not require specific intent as an element of the crime and in those cases the concept is not (or should not) be used. Diminished capacity can be argued as due to a specific mental condition or to drug or alcohol intoxication, as examples.

Exculpation

A term used as equivalent to legal insanity; that is, if insane, the defendant was exculpable or exculpated of the offense.

Federal Rule of Procedure 12.2C

A part of the Federal Evidence Code that details the fact that what is stated in a psychiatric/psychological evaluation can be used *only* for the formation of an opinion regarding mental state. It is not admissible to determine factual data (e.g., whether a person did or did not commit a particular offense).

Federal Rules of Evidence, 702-704

That part of the Federal Evidence Code which deals with the definition of an expert and the criteria for admissibility of expert testimony. While technically applicable only to Federal Courts, the Evidence Code in each state is largely based on the Federal Rules of Evidence.

Frye vs. U.S.

1923 case in which "general acceptance" (of methodology or theory) was the criterion for admissibility of expert testimony.

In-Camera Review

Literally an "in chamber" review by the judge to evaluate the merits of the Motion to Quash or Motion for a Protective Order or other legal matters.

Insanity Defense Reform Act of 1984

Part of the Comprehensive Crime Control Act passed by the U.S. Congress. Served to restrict the insanity defense to the cognitive prong of the A.L.I. test; eliminated the volitional prong; restricted usage to a defendant suffering from a "severe" mental disorder.

Mitigation

A concept referring to some condition that lessens a defendant's degree of guilt or blame-worthiness.

Motion to Quash or Motion for a Protective Order

Options that can be utilized by a mental health professional to avoid compliance with a subpoena when aspects of that subpoena demand material harmful to the relationship or threatening confidentiality. With or without an attorney, the practitioner can file such a Motion with the Clerk of the Court. This in effect puts the subpoena "on hold." The judge will then schedule a hearing on the Motion to Quash at which time the practitioner can detail the reasons for noncompliance. The judge will then issue a Court Order. The subpoena *is not* a Court Order. Once the Order is handed down, the practitioner should comply with the Orders or risk a Contempt of Court citation. There is *no* ethical violation in following a lawful Court Order, though there may be in a knee-jerk response to the subpoena.

Penultimate Issue

The level of inference just "below" the ultimate issue. Some forensic experts, for instance, while not stating that a given defendant fits the criteria for an absence of criminal responsibility (ultimate issue), may be willing to state that, based on the following psychological findings, the defendant "lacked substantial capacity to appreciate the wrongfulness of his behavior."

Product Test

A term derived from the *Durham* decision. A person is not criminally responsible if her or his crime is a product of a mental disease or defect (i.e., is directly caused by it).

Repressed Memories

A highly controversial area currently being hotly debated. Proponents believe that memories of childhood sexual abuse can be totally repressed and "recovered" through appropriate therapeutic techniques. Opponents question the reliability of such memories and suggest that such "memories" may actually be implanted by therapists.

Rules of Discovery

Rules, usually found within State or Federal Evidence Codes, which describe the circumstances under which materials (including expert opinions, data and reports) need to be revealed to opposing counsel.

Standard of Care

Concept relating to the level of practice of the average or relatively prudent practitioner; often used in malpractice litigation where the question is whether the practitioner deviated from a standard of care in a given field.

Substantial Capacity

Terminology used in a variety of criminal responsibility cases - first appearing in *McDonald* (312 F. 2d 844 [D.C. Circuit 1962]) - referring to an impairment less than an all or nothing, black or white concept embodied in earlier tests.

Third Party Data

Information gathered from independent sources to verify or disconfirm information provided by the defendant; an essential component of the assessment of malingering.

Ultimate Issue Testimony

An ongoing debate among forensic mental health professionals whether or not, in addition to presenting psychological data, the expert should render an opinion on the actual legal issues involved, for example, competent or not competent to stand trial.

Work Product

A term which describes what an expert may write or discuss with an attorney who has retained her or him, again, covered by attorney-client privilege unless waived.

SUBJECT AND
AUTHOR INDEX

CASE INDEX

Competency to Stand Trial Evaluations: A Manual for Practice

by Thomas Grisso

Of all the different forms of forensic mental health evaluations, the most frequently requested are competency to stand trial evaluations. Dr. Grisso, a preeminent forensic researcher and teacher, has put together a field tested manual of immense value. It is basic and straightforward, yet sufficiently complete to meet current legal requirements, professional standards, and the realistic demands of a forensic practice. Included are reviews of competency assessment instruments; discussions of ethical issues in competency evaluations of criminal defendants; case examples; and appendices detailing major legal cases, specialized evaluation tools, and reference citations.

Paperbound   1988   ISBN#: 0-943158-51-6

Instruments for Assessing Understanding & Appreciation of Miranda Rights

by Thomas Grisso

"Perhaps more than any other psychologist in the country, Dr. Grisso has contributed to advances in the field by promoting the need for scientifically grounded research and data-based forensic assessments. Dr. Grisso's groundbreaking research on the frequent inability of juveniles and adults to make legal Constitutional waivers of Miranda rights helped establish forensic psychology as a field that can and must rely upon objective data. This publication makes accessible to clinicians a number of forensic assessment instruments related to this area of psycho-legal practice.

"This material provides objective, data-based normative assessment instruments which, when used with other sources of information, provide essential information to both the forensic practitioner and the courts. The test materials and detailed scoring system are user friendly and contribute significantly to the reliability of these instruments. Sections describing the legal relevance of these instruments and the appellate decision citations related to Dr. Grisso's research should persuade both the clinician and the court that these assessment instruments meet both the Frye *and* Daubert *standards. The publication of these instruments as standardized tests represents a major contribution to the field of forensic assessment."*
Alan M. Goldstein, PhD, ABPP, Diplomate in Forensic Psychology,
Associate Professor of Psychology, John Jay College of Criminal Justice

When attorneys and courts have questions about the validity of criminal defendants' waiver of their Miranda rights at the time of police interrogation, forensic clinical examiners may be asked to assess defendants' capacities to understand and appreciate the "Miranda warnings" that they waived. This publication offers the only specialized instruments available to clinicians to assist them in these evaluations. Three of these instruments (Comprehension of Miranda Rights; Comprehension of Miranda Rights—Recognition; Comprehension of Miranda Vocabulary) allow the clinician to employ a multi-method approach to assessing understanding of the Miranda warnings, and a fourth (Function of Rights in Interrogation) examines the defendant's capacities to appreciate the significance of the rights in the context of police questioning, the attorney-client relationship, and court proceedings.

More ────────────▶

Based on the results of a comprehensive 3-year research study of their reliability and validity, these standardized instruments offer a structured, competency-based testing approach that employs objective scoring criteria, which permits the examiner to compare the performance of examinees to the performance of large normative samples of juvenile and adult offenders. A specially designed easel provides all of the stimuli and examiner prompts that are required for administration of the four instruments, and forms are available for recording and scoring responses. The manual offers a comprehensive description of the instruments, their development, tables of norms, and a discussion of the scientific and professional status of the instruments relevant for meeting legal criteria for admissibility as a basis for expert opinion in legal cases.

Flexible Binding Book	1998	1-56887-038-8
Spiralbound Test Easel	1998	1-56887-039-6
Package of 20 Test Forms	1998	1-56887-045-0

Forensic Evaluation of Juveniles

by Thomas Grisso

In recent years, juvenile courts and juvenile attorneys have come to rely heavily on mental health professionals for evaluations of youths in delinquency cases. Evaluation questions include the youth's competence to stand trial, competence to waive Miranda rights prior to giving a confession, the risk of future violence, rehabilitation needs, and whether he or she should be tried as a juvenile or an adult.

This book offers detailed guidance in performing evaluations for all of these purposes. Written for clinicians but also useful to lawyers and others dealing with such evaluations, each chapter carefully defines the legal and clinical questions for a particular type of evaluation, describes the evaluation process in detail, reviews relevant assessment methods, and discusses issues in interpretation and testimony. The descriptions are guided by current legal requirements and the latest research results in the behavioral and medical sciences, blended with practical advice derived from the author's 25 years of experience in the forensic evaluation of juveniles. The introductory chapter examines the historical, legal, scientific, and professional contexts in which clinicians engage in forensic evaluations of juveniles, and the closing chapter offers a comprehensive review of ethical and professional issues in juvenile forensic practice.

"Whenever you crack the spine of a book by Thomas Grisso, you do so in anticipation of excellence. In **Forensic Evaluation of Juveniles**, *Grisso outdoes even himself. Anchored both in state-of-the-art developmental research and in far-ranging clinical experience, this is the most authoritative work on the assessment of adolescents for the courts ever written. The book's timing is perfect and its impact on the field is sure to be immense."*
John Monahan, PhD, Doherty Professor of Law, Professor of Psychology and Legal Medicine, University of Virginia

"Grisso has done it again. **Forensic Evaluation of Juveniles** *is a masterful blend of practical utility with relevant theory and research, with something to offer everyone from the beginner to the experienced forensic clinician. The most important mental health issues in juvenile law - transfer, rehabilitation, violence risk, competence for trial, and competence to waive* Miranda *- are addressed in a way that is certain to improve clinical forensic practice and, ultimately, the product that is provided to courts, attorneys, and agencies."*
Kirk Heilbrun, PhD, Professor and Co-Director, Law-Psychology Program, Allegheny University of Health Sciences/Villanova School of Law

"In his typically unassuming style, Dr. Grisso presents a book which on the surface is a straightforward manual for clinical consultation practice with juvenile defendants. In this guise, the book provides detailed, careful, and sound advice on conducting evaluations in a variety of delinquency contexts. This book will set standards which should significantly improve consultative practice with courts and youth corrections agencies."

Richard Barnum, MD, Director, Boston Juvenile Court Clinic

Hardbound   1998   ISBN#: 1-56887-037-X

Resources For Assessing Competence to Consent to Treatment

by Thomas Grisso and Paul S. Appelbaum

One of the most challenging tasks facing clinicians today is the assessment of patients' capacities to consent to treatment. The protection of a patient's right to decide, as well as the protection of incompetent patients from the potential harm of their decisions, rests largely on clinicians' abilities to judge patients' capacities to decide what treatment they will receive.

The materials described below are the product of an 8-year study of patients' capacities to make treatment decisions - the most comprehensive research of its kind.

The book, *Assessing Competence to Consent to Treatment: A Guide for Physicians and Other Health Professionals*, describes the place of competence in the doctrine of informed consent, analyzes the elements of decision making, and shows how assessments of competence to consent to treatment can be conducted within varied general medical and psychiatric treatment settings. Numerous case studies illustrate real-life applications of the concepts and methods discussed.

The *Manual* for the *MacArthur Competence Assessment Tool for Treatment (MacCAT-T)* is a large-format and examiner-friendly field manual for conducting actual competency assessments.

The *MacCAT-T Record Form* is well designed for recording, rating, and summarizing patient responses.

The MacCAT-T video demonstrates an actual administration of the *MacArthur Competence Assessment Tool for Treatment (MacCAT-T)* with discussion, comments, and annotations by Drs. Grisso and Appelbaum.

Book: *Assessing Competence to Consent to Treatment:*
A Guide for Physicians and Other Health Professionals
5-1/2" x 8-1/2" Hardbound   1998   ISBN#: 0-19-510372-6

Manual: *MacArthur Competence Assessment Tool for Treatment (MacCAT-T)*
8-1/2" x 11"   Paperback   1998   ISBN#: 1-56887-041-8

Forms: *MacCAT-T Record Forms*
Package of 10   1998   ISBN#: 1-56887-042-6

Video: *Administering the MacArthur Competence Assessment Tool for Treatment (MacCAT-T)*
VHS   1999   ISBN#: 1-56887-043-4

More ──────────────▶

Assessing Allegations of Child Sexual Abuse

by Kathryn Kuehnle

"This book is destined to become the defacto standard reference for child sexual abuse assessment. It will be widely used by attorneys and forensic experts to review and assess the thoroughness and scientific validity of forensic child sexual abuse evaluations. Any clinician not familiar with the content will be unprepared for cross-examination and subject to considerable embarrassment on the witness stand."
   Gerald P. Koocher, PhD, Harvard Medical School,
   Reviewing in *American Psychology-Law Society News*

"For psychologists concerned with assessing alleged child sexual abuse, Dr. Kuehnle has written an extremely informative and useful text that combines sound scholarship with sophisticated clinical insight. Based on her extensive experience in evaluating alleged victims and perpetrators of abuse and a thorough review of the relevant literature, she gives clarity to a broad range of issues raised by these cases and provides detailed guidelines for conducting reliable assessments of the parties to them."
   Irving B. Weiner, PhD, Tampa, FL

Evaluating allegations of child sexual abuse is a complicated task in which evaluators *can* do great harm to individuals and families if they ignore ethical principles or scientific knowledge. In this critically acclaimed work, Dr. Kathryn Kuehnle provides essential information on ethically and professionally appropriate procedures for conducting such evaluations.

In his review, Dr. Stephen J. Ceci comments on the author's "uncommonly good common sense" for guiding the reader "through the clinical, scientific, and ethical minefields awaiting all who become involved in child abuse allegations." Dr. Mark D. Everson praises the way in which Dr. Kuehnle "skillfully highlighted what is relevant, what is important, and what is useful for informing practice from the empirical literature."

If you are currently evaluating child sexual abuse allegations (or considering conducting such evaluations), this book is likely to become the most valuable resource in your professional library.

Hardbound   1996   ISBN#: 1-56887-009-4

Tarasoff *and Beyond:*
Legal and Clinical Considerations
In the Treatment of Life-Endangering Patients

by Leon VandeCreek and Samuel Knapp

Reviews the landmark *Tarasoff* "duty to warn" decision, subsequent and recent court rulings, and their legal and clinical implications. Focuses on homicidal, suicidal, and child-abusing clients. Details ethical and legal responsibilities regarding AIDS patients, incompetent drivers, disclosure of past crimes, and other critical issues. Recommends steps for minimizing liability risks while still providing appropriate treatment.

Paperbound   1993   ISBN#: 0-943158-91-5

Psychology, Psychiatry, and the Law: A Clinical and Forensic Handbook

Charles Patrick Ewing, Editor

Psychology and psychiatry are discussed in relation to criminal justice, civil commitment, family law, tort law, and workers' compensation. Other sections cover such topics as being an expert witness, use of the behavioral sciences in jury selection and truth detection, and legal regulation of mental health practice.

Twenty contributions including: Evaluating Potentially Violent Persons (John Monahan), Sentencing Guidelines (Jolene Galegher and John S. Carroll), Civil Commitment (Robert D. Miller), Child Custody Disputes (Andrew P. Musetto), Child Abuse and Neglect Cases (Melvin J. Guyer and Peter Ash), Personal Injury Litigation (Harold H. Smith, Jr.), Products Liability Litigation (Martin I. Kurke), Workers' Compensation (Herbert N. Weissman), Expertise on the Witness Stand (Stanley L. Brodsky and Norman G. Poythress), Eyewitness Testimony (David F. Hall and Elizabeth F. Loftus), Jury Selection (Diane R. Follingstad), and more.

Paperbound   1985   ISBN#: 0-943158-11-7

AUDIOCASSETTE TAPES:

Ten Commandments for the Expert Witness by Charles Patrick Ewing. Dr. Ewing outlines the 10 basic steps to becoming a successful expert witness.
40 minutes   1985   ISBN#: 0-943158-12-5

Preparing for a Forensic Mental Health Practice by Thomas Grisso. This audiotape will help you evaluate your preparedness for conducting forensic evaluations, and provide steps to enhance your skills.
60 minutes   1988   ISBN#: 0-943158-27-3

FOR CURRENT PRICING AND ORDERING INFORMATION

Phone: 1-800-443-3364   Fax: 1-941-343-9201

Email: mail@prpress.com   Website: http://www.prpress.com

Write: Professional Resource Press,
PO Box 15560, Sarasota FL 34277-1560

If you found this book useful . . .

You might want to know more about our other titles.

If you would like to receive our latest catalog, please return this form:

Name: _____
(Please Print)

Address: _____

Address: _____

City/State/Zip: _____
This is my ☐home ☐office

Telephone: (_____) _____

I am a:

_____ Psychologist   _____ Attorney
_____ Psychiatrist   _____ Other: _____

I am interested in:

_____ Forensic Titles
_____ Clinical Titles
_____ Other: _____

◆   ◆   ◆

Professional Resource Press
P.O. Box 15560
Sarasota, FL 34277-1560

Telephone: 1-800-443-3364
Fax: 1-941-343-9201
Email: mail@prpress.com
Website: http://www.prpress.com